PORTSMOUTH

FOOTBALL CLUB

2002/03
POMPEY'S RISE
TO THE
PREMIERSHIP

PORTSMOUTH
FOOTBALL CLUB

2002/03
POMPEY'S RISE
TO THE
PREMIERSHIP

RICHARD OWEN

TEMPUS

Front cover: Paul Merson, Pompey club captain, sums up the feeling enjoyed by everyone connected with the club in a magnificent season. (Picture by Mike Jones)

Frontispiece: 4 March 2003 – when Fratton Park moved to Selhurst.

First published 2003

Tempus Publishing Limited
The Mill, Brimscombe Port,
Stroud, Gloucestershire, GL5 2QG

British Library Cataloguing in Publication Data.
A catalogue record for this book is available from the British Library.

ISBN 0 7524 2935 3

Typesetting and origination by Tempus Publishing Limited
Printed in Great Britain by Midway Colour Print, Wiltshire

Acknowledgements

In compiling this book, the photography of Mike Jones played a large part. Aged only eighteen, I am sure we will all see a great deal more of Mike's pictures in years to come. Words and pictures go together and without Mike's acute skill of capturing crisp action shots and his ability to seize the moment, the book would be incomplete. Having been involved with the Portsmouth FC matchday programme for the past twenty-five years, Mike's photographs, in particular his action shots, are the best I have ever seen.

I would like to thank Peter Storrie, Paul Weld, Jason Stone and Tara Snowden; all at Portsmouth Football Club, whose help, guidance and assistance in the preparation of this book was essential. I would also like to thank the directors of Portsmouth FC for giving an official endorsement to this publication and for allowing the club badge to be reproduced.

Thanks are also due to Mark Storey at *The News, Portsmouth* for the occasional checking of facts, and Pompey supporters Steve Byrne, Paul Craven, Mike Gardner, Richard Holledge, Ken Fisher, Alan Jenkins, Steve Launay, Mark Haslam and Paul Till, whose regular checks on my sanity and health were greatly appreciated.

I would like to acknowledge the personnel department of my employer Hampshire Constabulary and, in particular, my line manager Hillary Jefferson, who granted me unpaid leave to write the book.

Thanks also to James Howarth and Becky Gadd at Tempus Publishing, for their advice and patience, and finally to my father and mother, for their moral support and supply of sustenance to keep body and soul together.

About the author

Born on a wet Monday morning, just after Ron Saunders had scored at the weekend against Cardiff City in November 1959, Richard was raised in Cosham and educated at Highbury School and Portsmouth Grammar School. It was during these years that he developed a penchant for writing and he became a collector of football programmes from the age of ten.

Taken by his father to see Charlton Athletic at Fratton Park on Boxing Day 1965, he became a passionate Pompey supporter following in his grandfather's and father's footsteps. Like many, he remained unswervingly loyal during Pompey's nadir in the mid-1970s and has missed only a handful of first-team away games since 1977, spectating at over 109 different English League grounds with Pompey; 1984 was the last time he missed an away match. Richard's absence from his 'second home' at Fratton Park has been registered just once since 1973 – due to major surgery in 1997.

Richard has contributed to the official Portsmouth FC match programme for the past twenty-five years and since becoming the club's official honorary historian, he has written several publications, which include *An A-Z of Pompey Legends* (*The News, Portsmouth*, 1993), and was co-writer, with Peter Jeffs and Colin Farmery, of *The Official Centenary Pictorial History of Portsmouth FC* and *Portsmouth FC, Official Centenary Team Collection* (both Bishops Printers Ltd, 1998).

Having painstakingly amassed one of the largest, near-complete collections of Portsmouth home and away matchday programmes (dating back to 1946) known to be in existence, together with an extensive collection of Pompey memorabilia,

Richard hopes to be in a position to assist in establishing a club museum to celebrate Pompey's illustrious history when Fratton Park is redeveloped in 2005.

Richard is also a member of the Ex-Pompey FC Professionals Committee who voluntarily help to organise bi-annual reunions, and through the co-operation of Portsmouth FC, he arranges hospitality for ex-Pompey players at Fratton Park on match days.

Introduction

When Pompey dispatched Wimbledon 4-1 at Fratton Park in September 2002 to amass 7 wins on the bounce, everyone sensed it was going to be a special season. It was then that I decided to write this book. Pompey supporters have been weaned on a diet of dour struggle during most of the last ten seasons. There have been too many nerve-jangling finales, involving must-win end-of-season fixtures against Huddersfield, Bradford and Barnsley. Pompey had the worst away record of the 92 clubs in the Football League over a five-year span. So, what a blast of fresh air this season has been: it has been all about waking brightly, going to work with a smiling face, and listening to non-football friends and neighbours talking about Pompey. Pompey fans everywhere have had a spring in their step during this overdue season of success.

Very few of us could have imagined what a sensational season it would turn out to be though, even after that Wimbledon match. With all the previous drama of near relegations, going into administration, several changes of manager and failed ground moves, this season's 46-match marathon was entirely different – a fascinating and enjoyable experience. Season ticket sales rocketed and spare tickets were like gold dust. Pompey's army of fanatical support could hardly comprehend the incredible turnaround in results. Our dear old Fratton Park stadium was the place to be, described by Simon Inglis in his excellent 1983 publication *The Football Grounds of England & Wales* as ' ... a northern ground, inland and serious with stands which need to be filled with people'. They certainly were this season, thanks to the hard work of Elaine Giles, Lynn Wells, Malcolm Handley and all the other staff in the Pompey ticket office.

But they could not have sold those tickets without the two men who are ultimately responsible. Firstly, the chairman Milan Mandaric, whose money and dogged ambition has made a dream come true for all of us. Minus our Serbia-born American leader, it could be argued that there might not be a Portsmouth FC today, let alone one in the Premier League. Secondly, his wise move in employing former Bournemouth and West Ham United manager Harry Redknapp to take over as manager proved to be the masterstroke for a long overdue upturn in this old football club's proud history. Having watched most of Pompey's home and away games as director of football during the 2001/02 season, Harry's seasoned eye for a good player – and his cunning and guile in the transfer market – resulted in one of the best double acts of finance and integrity the club has ever seen in its 105-year existence.

This book relives, match by match, what was an astonishing season, created by the many players Harry brought in alongside the few he inherited and kept. He recruited the wise experience and deep knowledge of assistant manager Jim Smith and first-team coach Kevin Bond, which gave the Pompey management team an auspicious trio streets ahead of others in the League. With an encyclopaedic knowledge of the player market, both at home and abroad, Harry recruited a United Nations of footballers, including Gianluca Festa, Arjan De Zeeuw, Lassina Diabate and Vincent Pericard to play alongside the massively influential free transfer signing Paul Merson. Adding the bargain purchases of Hayden Foxe (£200,000), Matthew Taylor (£750,000) and Svetoslav Todorov (£750,000), Harry had the nucleus of a special side – one which was to have the city buzzing with a level of excitement not experienced since those back-to-back Championship successes in the early post-war years.

Several club records were broken as this diary of the season reveals. Surprisingly, given his managerial reign at the top of the League for the majority of the season, Harry won only a single Division One Manager of the Month award. So perhaps it was natural justice that Harry Redknapp was ultimately crowned Division One Manager of the Year in May 2003 – a prestigious award of achievement for a club turned round on its axis in just thirteen months.

One of several unheralded facts of the season was the small squad of players Harry worked with – on many occasions, he had only sixteen fit players to take on the away coach. Some of the media trumpeted the 'vast sums' he had spent assembling his table-topping squad, which was quite incorrect when the total added up to approximately £2.2m; a moderate sum in comparison to Leicester City, who eventually finished 6 points adrift of Pompey. Indeed, if this was the price of a ticket to the Premiership and all its high-profile wealth, this sum must be considered paltry. Tribute must also be paid here to Pompey chief executive Peter Storrie, who carefully managed the club's expenditure and, alongside Harry, negotiated with players' agents.

Harry and Jim's joint expertise reached its zenith at critical junctures during the season when the team was shored up with the experience of Steve Stone (free transfer), the match-winning style of Tim Sherwood (free) and the lightning pace and shooting of Yakubu Aiyegbeni (loan) that ultimately sealed our success. The wage-bill did not suffer as no fewer than seven other players were released on loan elsewhere.

The players who gelled together so quickly to start the season in magnificent style continued to work all season as a committed unit. Below stairs, in the inner sanctum, Gary Sadler and Chris Neville grafted very hard to get players fit – clearly the home-made rice pudding and Jaffa cakes diet idea worked! Kit-man Kevin McCormack, the Welsh giant of Persil-land, always spoke well of a happy atmosphere among the lads, at home or away.

A total of 16 clean sheets and a record 97 goals scored were the basis of Pompey's successful bid for the Division One title. Furthermore, not a single player was sent off all season – that hasn't happened for twenty-two years and was undoubtedly another factor behind Pompey's surge to the top. It all adds up to a remarkable story, even more so considering the maximum ground capacity of 19,600 limited the club's income to be earned from gate receipts.

Pompey's success was celebrated far and wide throughout the season, abroad and at home. For my small part, the six *Football Mails* I sent out every Sunday to Overton, Malvern, Rossendale, Barrow-in-Furness, Forfar and Askeaton reached exiled supporters who drank in every word and picture as they could not get to

Harry Redknapp hails a remarkable season upon clinching the Division One Championship.

every game. Hordes of fans at the twenty-four grounds Pompey graced were a sight to behold, and they became the envy of opposing managers and supporters alike when they heard them sing to register as Pompey's twelfth man.

When Pompey won promotion from the Fourth Division on goal difference in 1980, friends said to me then, amid the large jubilant crowds, 'What will it be like when we really win something?'. The answer, twenty-three years later, was the party of all parties at the civic reception held on Sunday 11 May. An amazing 45,000 people packed Southsea Common at the foot of many Portsmouth streets showered in colourful joy. Unlike some others, this city knows how to celebrate success. With its Royal Naval homecomings as a yardstick, I am told by my elders that scenes in Portsmouth on 11 May reminded them of a royal visit or VE Day in 1945.

In the interests of accuracy, details have been authenticated by reference to press reports of the games where my own notes, made avidly and mentally in each match, were missing. In what was the most memorable season in my lifetime of supporting Pompey, I hope you enjoy reading the memories as much as I did writing them.

Richard Owen
May 2003

DEBUT DAY

Date: Saturday 10 August 2002   **Referee:** Dermot Gallagher (Oxfordshire)
Attendance: 18,510   **Man of the Match:** Vincent Pericard

The start of Pompey's fifteenth consecutive season in Division One provided a large Fratton Park crowd, with no fewer than eight new players making their Pompey debut, although loan signing Deon Burton had played for Pompey before in the 1990s. Those eight new faces that day included Shaka Hislop, who won a race against injury to start in goal, Hayden Foxe and Arjan De Zeeuw, who partnered each other in the centre of defence, and Carl Robinson, who came in for pre-season injury-hit Richard Hughes. Matthew Taylor, a £750,000 snip from Luton Town, also pulled on a blue shirt for the first time, together with Vincent Pericard, a year-long loan signing from Juventus. Paul Merson led the virtually new team out of the tunnel as captain, followed by last-minute loan signing Deon Burton from Derby County. There was no room for Mark Burchill, who was on the bench.

No stranger to the immaculate Fratton turf was referee Dermot Gallagher, who blew his whistle to signal the start of the 2002/03 season, which heralded much promise after an encouraging pre-season. A frantic start by both sides followed with tackles flying in. Visitors Forest, captained by veteran Des Walker and one of the sides tipped for promotion, showed some lively moves, but a crude challenge on Pompey's Eddie Howe provided the first scare of the season as he limped off to be replaced by Linvoy Primus.

With 46 matches in the marathon English season, winning the first is always regarded as a dream start and the noisy crowd, containing over 8,000 season-ticket holders, were treated to the first goal of the campaign after just 8 minutes. Nigel Quashie got away down the left flank towards the Milton End where he crossed the ball to Pericard, who failed to meet the midfielder's pass but Deon Burton, who had only arrived at the ground from Derby fourteen hours previously, was unmarked to fire home from 6 yards. His arms-outstretched celebration beneath the South Stand signalled an eruption of noise from the old ground.

Nottingham Forest midfielder Riccardo Scimeca caused Pompey some problems and provided two clear attempts to score, but Pompey's defence soaked up the pressure to entertain the crowd with some good moves forward too in an entertaining game. On the stroke of half-time, Linvoy Primus and Gary O'Neil engineered a chance which gave Vincent Pericard his first goal. A flick over the top of Forest's defence found O'Neil, whose first-time cross was met by Pericard, who buried a powerful header from 6 yards.

In the second half, Pericard continued to cause problems and so, too, did Forest substitute Jack Lester, who struck a shot from a narrow angle which beat Shaka Hislop, but Arjan De Zeeuw recovered well to head the ball off the line. Matthew Taylor delighted Pompey fans with some fine runs down the left-hand flank, and he capped a fine afternoon for all the Pompey debutants with a 20-yard shot, which was blocked by Forest 'keeper Ward.

Portsmouth 2   **Nottingham Forest 0**
Burton
Pericard

Portsmouth FC directors Fred Dinenage and Terry Brady with chairman Milan Mandaric are all smiles with the first 3 points.

The first day of the season had brought 3 points, a near full house, despite the Eastern Road being closed, a clean sheet, an entertaining game and both strikers on target. Paul Merson, one of many deft signings by Harry Redknapp, showed his potential and only tired in the last 15 minutes, playing his first full game since March for Aston Villa.

Portsmouth: Hislop, Foxe, De Zeeuw, Howe, Taylor, Robinson, Quashie, O'Neil, Merson, Pericard, Burton. Subs: Kawaguchi, Primus, Crowe, Barrett, Burchill.
Nottingham Forest: Ward, Hjelde, Walker, Thompson, Hall, Williams, Prutton, Louis-Jean, Brennan, Scimeca, Johnson. Subs: Roche, Lester, Harewood, Reid, Westcarr.

Date: Tuesday 13 August 2002
Attendance: 16,093

Referee: Anthony Bates (Stoke-on-Trent)
Man of the Match: Paul Merson/Hayden Foxe

Ask any regular travelling Pompey fan which ground they least enjoy going to each season and nine out of ten would say Bramall Lane. There are several reasons for this – the main one is that Pompey have not won there since November 1955. In addition to that, controversy has reigned each time Pompey have played at the ground in their last few visits, including a Pompey player ending up in hospital.

When the fixture list was issued in June, groans could be heard everywhere at the reading of Pompey's first away game of the new season at Bramall Lane, an evening match with a tedious journey to boot. With United's well-worn pitch, fervent home support and manager Neil Warnock's aggressive style ingrained into his squad, there could be no ground in England where a win bonus was more guaranteed for the home club.

But for all that, Sheffield United are regarded as another underachieving club in Division One. They enjoy large crowds, decent support similar to Pompey and Wolves, but they are rarely in the top three as they should be. On a warm August evening in South Yorkshire, the Pompey team who took to the field where so many had previously failed, contained only two players – Primus and Quashie – who had played in the 4-3 defeat of six months previously. The rest were new and were not concerned about Pompey's poor record there.

Playing in their smart gold away strip, Pompey rewarded the 939 Pompey fans who made the long journey with a treat of quality football to ruffle United supporters' hopes of an expected first home win of the season. Plenty of chances were created in the match, with Deon Burton admitting he should have netted a hat-trick, but in textbook style it was Sheffield who opened the scoring. Matthew Taylor, who had an eventful game, miscued a clearance from an area of relative safety down near the corner flag, which conveniently sped out to Peter Ndlovu, who wrongfooted the Pompey defence and placed a fierce shot past Shaka Hislop.

Shaka, shaken but not stirred, then kept Pompey in the game with a superb low one-handed save to his left to deny Michael Tonge and, minutes later, his quick thinking denied Steve Yates from close range. Those saves provided a boost for Pompey to step up a gear and show the Sheffield fans reading their programme notes that Pompey were going to be the surprise team of the division this season. Incisive, quality football flowed from Gary O'Neil, Nigel Quashie and Paul Merson, who piled pressure on the United goal. On 25 minutes, Pompey were level, Merson flicking a super shot over the Blades defence, which Deon Burton collected neatly, before skipping around 'keeper Paddy Kenny and stroking home his second goal in two games. For a player not 100 per cent fit and without any pre-season games under his belt, it was impressive stuff.

The second half produced excellent defending from De Zeeuw and Foxe, whose new partnership boded well for the future. Pompey's diamond-shaped four-man

Sheffield United 1	Portsmouth 1
Ndlovu	*Burton*

Deon Burton rounds the United 'keeper to score his second goal in 2 matches and Pompey's equaliser.

midfield coped admirably with United's runs, and Merson was unlucky with a lob which Kenny just managed to claw out of the air. With 9 minutes left, Pompey nearly rocked the record books with a sweet Merson pass from the outside of his boot which sent substitute Todorov on his way. His low cross was perfect for Burton, just 6 yards out, to put away, but he sidefooted over the bar.

It was rough. This was Pompey's best performance in decades at Bramall Lane and they deserved the win after forty-seven years of struggle, but a scoring draw was a vast improvement and the quality of their performance gave Pompey's noisy support plenty to talk about on their way back down the M1.

Sheffield United: Kenny, Kozluk, Ullathorne, Yates, Murphy, M. Brown, Ndlovu, Jaglelka, Tonge, Asaba, Onoura. Subs: Doan, McGovern, Peschisillido, Javary.
Portsmouth: Hislop, Primus, Foxe, De Zeeuw, Taylor, O'Neil, Robinson, Merson, Quashie, Burton, Pericard. Subs: Todorov, Hughes, Burchill.

Date: Saturday 17 August 2002
Attendance: 18,315

Referee: Steven Dunn (Bristol)
Man of the Match: Jason Crowe

Football in mid-August can often be uncomfortable with southern temperatures. In the middle of a heatwave on the South Coast, even Portsmouth near the sea was boiling. So a trip to the bricks and mortar suburbs of south London with the temperature in the 90s was the last place the Pompey team and fans wanted to be. Side-road tarmac was melting on the approaches to Selhurst Park before the game, and the majority of Pompey's massive travelling army of 3,688 fans who filled the Arthur Wait stand were shirtless. Few of them would have predicted the drama that was about to unfold.

Pompey, unchanged from Sheffield, faced an unbeaten Palace side containing former Pompey captain Shaun Derry and debut man Dele Adebola. Vincent Pericard fluffed two chances fed from Merson early in the first half, only to collapse clutching his hip, and he eventually limped off to be replaced by Todorov. Although Pompey had more of the possession, they were creating very few chances and the game turned into a scrappy, disjointed affair, with even the referee taking water when the ball was out of play to cope with the energy-sapping conditions.

However, in the 5-minute spell before half-time, Palace were suddenly 2-0 up. A mistake by Quashie saw his crossfield ball go straight to Dougie Freedman, who raced towards goal through several gold shirts and cut across the area before slotting a shot into the top corner. Then Granville whipped in a cross from the left for Popovic to bury with a firm header at the Sainsbury's End. Pompey were all over the place and went in for the break lucky not to have conceded three.

The old cliché of a 'game of two halves' was perfectly orchestrated by manager Harry Redknapp. Removing Gary O'Neil and Carl Robinson, he switched to a wing-back formation with Jason Crowe on the right and Richard Hughes partnering Paul Merson. Midway through the second half, Pompey fans were still stunned, with Todorov, Merson and Taylor all testing Matt Clarke in the Palace goal without success. Gary Butterfield then nearly finished the game at 3-0 when his free-kick hit the post. Yellow cards for Primus and De Zeeuw added to the misery.

But on 68 minutes, the game changed dramatically, and the next 5 minutes were about to be recorded in Pompey folklore. Pompey won a corner at the Sainsbury's End, which turned the game. Matthew Taylor fed a great cross for Aussie Hayden Foxe to head home his first Pompey goal. Within 60 seconds, Pompey were level. Palace lost possession from the restart, Taylor charged down the left wing, the Palace defenders were caught ball-watching, and Taylor's low cross was stabbed into the net by Crowe to make it 2-2.

Pompey had Palace reeling. Pompey fans were jumping up and down, forgetting how hot they were. Just 3 minutes later, they were in ecstasy. A man who had only scored once in three years for the Blues, substitute Jason Crowe, won the ball down the right and charged forward into the box to feed Burton. Deon calmly poked the

---

Crystal Palace 2
Freedman
Popovic

Portsmouth 3
Foxe
Crowe (2)

Super sub Jason Crowe helped turned the game around completely with two second-half goals.

ball around Clarke before laying a pass square to Crowe who, despite several Palace players around him, astutely stroked the ball into the top corner.

Pompey's comeback at Palace two years previously had been good, but this was incredible. Selhurst Park, renowned for its difficult location and regular defeats for Pompey fans, was now the scene for remarkable recoveries. In 2000, Pompey had come back from 2-0 down to win away for the first time in thirty-seven years. In 2001, they had turned a 3-goal second-half deficit against Wimbledon into a point. The intense heat was swept aside; Jason Crowe had to apologise to his Palace-supporting brother for the damage he'd caused, and Merson spoke of his first 'wall of sound' experience of Pompey's loud away support. It was only the third time that Pompey had scored 3 goals in 5 minutes in the last twenty years too.

Crystal Palace: Clarke, Powell, Austin, Popovic, Mullins, Butterfield, Granville, Thomson, Derry, Riihilahti, Adebola, Freeman. Subs: Austin, Fleming, Kabba, Kolinko, Black.
Portsmouth: Hislop, Primus, Foxe, De Zeeuw, Taylor, O'Neil, Robinson, Merson, Quashie, Burton, Pericard. Subs: Todorov, Hughes, Crowe, Burchill, Kawaguchi.

Date: Saturday 24 August 2002
Attendance: 17,901

Referee: Mark Cooper (Walsall)
Man of the Match: Paul Merson

A scorching hot Bank Holiday weekend would signal for many people the garden, the beach or a trip abroad. However, the place to be was Fratton Park. If Pompey's excellent start to the season was still not believed by doubters, this game cemented it. Manager Harry Redknapp made four changes to the winning side at Palace from the previous week: Gianluca Festa made his debut in place of Primus; Jason Crowe came in at right-back as a reward for his two goals at Palace; Richard Hughes came into the midfield for Robinson; and Todorov replaced the injured Pericard.

The first half showed Pompey in confident mood, creating several chances, and it appeared to be a case of when Pompey would score, rather than if. Watford's first effort took 20 minutes, and when Todorov fired close with a spectacular 30-yard volley on the half-hour, the half-dressed crowd became frustrated. However, in a 5-minute spell either side of half-time, 3 goals brought the match to life. Paul Merson sent a brilliant pass down the right for Jason Crowe, who cut around Gayle and charged into the box, only to be upended by Gayle's boot. Penalty! Merson took it for his first Pompey goal, striking high past Chamberlain into the Milton net. In injury time, Merson was again the provider. His pass found Burton on the right, who flicked in a low cross for Todorov, whose quick-thinking shot on the turn flew into the bottom left-hand corner, 2-0.

The second half could not come soon enough. Todorov, whose fitness had visibly improved since his signing the previous March, showed great power in pulling away from Cox to slip a superb ball through to Deon Burton, who had only the 'keeper to beat. Showing his Premiership experience and great composure, he steadied himself and rifled a left-foot shot across Chamberlain's goal into the far corner. 3-0 – sunny day, clean sheet. What was going on?

Merson then unleashed a 20-yard drive which hit the bar to crown a wonderful performance, and the Fratton End were crowing his name long before the end. Watford's first shot on target was 5 minutes from the end, and Nielsen's sending-off for foul and abusive language completed the misery for a poor-looking Watford side, who looked well-beaten and fortunate not to have conceded more. For Pompey, Festa gave a promising debut and Merson's creativity stood out.

The League table after the match showed that Norwich and Coventry City shared 10 points with Pompey at the top, which boosted Pompey's team confidence even more in readiness for the long trip east to Cleethorpes just 48 hours away.

Portsmouth 3
Merson (penalty)
Todorov
Burton

Watford 0

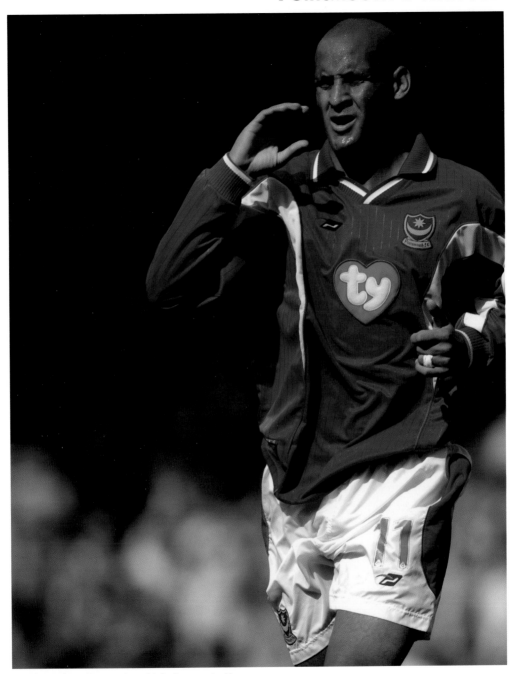

Nigel Quashie: 'Bazza, gissa drink. I'm gagging!'

Portsmouth: Hislop, Festa, Foxe, De Zeeuw, Crowe, Taylor, Hughes, Quashie, Merson, Burton, Todorov. Subs: Burchill, O'Neil, Robinson, Kawaguchi, Primus.

Watford: Chamberlain, Cox, Dyche, Gayle, Ardley, Robinson, Nielsen, Hyde, Hand, T. Smith, Webber. Subs: Doyley, Vernazza, Glass, Lee, Foley.

EAST COAST EXCESS

Date: Monday 26 August 2002
Attendance: 5,770

Referee: Matt Messias (York)
Man of the Match: Hayden Foxe

With Bramall Lane out of the way, another equally dreaded ground to visit early on the fixture list was Blundell Park in the windy wastes of Lincolnshire's east coast. How people can cope living here, I cannot comprehend. No matter what time of year Pompey play Grimsby, the weather is always wintry. We left Portsmouth in sunshine and when we arrived in Cleethorpes on a Bank Holiday Monday lunchtime in August, it was raining. The perpetual bitter wind which blows off the east coast into the ground, coupled with an overcast sky and chilly temperature, made us wish for the Sports Report signature tune on Radio Five to come round as quickly as possible.

Under Bobby Campbell and Alan Ball, Pompey won matches at Blundell Park – very few have seen a win bonus since. Grimsby Town on paper is a match that Pompey are expected to win each season, but they seldom do, often beaten by a club surviving on tiny crowds and even smaller resources. The match announcer cheered up the 1,061 hardy Pompey fans by welcoming them to the town, but that's where the hospitality ended. Large sections of the crowd were very partisan.

Grimsby, without a win since the season started, huffed and puffed into Pompey with resolve but still only managed three shots on target in 90 minutes. Pompey's back three of Foxe, De Zeeuw and Festa never looked threatened the whole match. Grimsby's nearest chance came from Crystal Palace loan forward Steve Kabba, who sprawled in the box near Festa but merely got a yellow card for diving.

The match was largely uneventful for a Bank Holiday crowd; the Grimsby manager Paul Groves decided to play Kabba on his own up front, supported by two wide players, which resulted in Pompey's play being ultra-defensive. Paul Merson was visiting Grimsby for the first time in his long career. He showed his familiar running skills with ball-chasing, and he connected well to create four clear chances for Burton and Todorov.

Hayden Foxe was the Man of the Match with excellent self-assured defending; Hislop had virtually nothing to do. The only goal of the game came late – again, something rarely in Pompey's script. Deon Burton had limped off with a knock to be replaced by Mark Burchill. Still far from even 90 per cent fit from his knee surgery, Burchill netted a well-taken goal on 85 minutes. Hislop's long clearance was flicked on by Todorov to Burchill, who swivelled away from his marker and walloped a 20-yard left-footer low into the net past Coyne, much to the joy of the Pompey fans behind the Clock End.

Although four yellow cards were issued – to Hislop, De Zeeuw, Todorov and Harper – the win was priceless. Grimsby tried their best, and it is never the most inspiring of places to roll up sleeves and grind out a result. The victory ended a bad run of defeats for Pompey in this depressing town and continued their excellent start to the season. By the time Pompey supporters were well on the M180 west-bound,

Grimsby Town 0   Portsmouth 1
                                          Burchill

Pompey's Mark Burchill scored the winning goal to place Pompey at the top of the division.

radio news declared Pompey were top of the League for the first time since April 1993, by virtue of others losing, which just summed up an odd day all round, but a happy one nevertheless. Very few of the 1,061 supporters who watched Pompey at Grimsby would have wagered they would still be top, unmoved, 9 months later.

Grimsby Town: Coyne, McDermott, Gallimore, Groves, Chettle, Cooke, Coldicott, Ford, Campbell, Kabba, Barnard. Subs: Robinson, Rowan, Ward, Bolder, Hughes.
Portsmouth: Hislop, Festa, Foxe, De Zeeuw, Crowe, Taylor, Hughes, Quashie, Merson, Burton, Todorov. Subs: Burchill, Harper, Robinson, Primus, Kawaguchi.

Date: Saturday 31 August 2002
Attendance: 19,031

Referee: Steven Bennett (Orpington)
Man of the Match: Nigel Quashie

Local derbies can often be disappointing, stale affairs. This one was far from that in the rare battle of Hampshire v. Sussex. Tickets for the match were all sold by the morning after the Grimsby win and with the sun shining and Pompey chasing their best-ever start to a season, appetite for the match was strong. Brighton's all-black change strip matched their form, with 3 straight defeats behind them. Typically, there were plenty of club connections with Pompey's former reserve-team manager Martin Hinshelwood, now Brighton manager, fielding three ex-Pompey players in his ageing Seagulls side – goalkeeper Andy Petterson and defenders Guy Butters and Robbie Pethick. Brighton's goal supremo Bobby Zamora was injured.

Pompey, unchanged for the third game on the trot, opened strongly and were ahead in just 3 minutes, kicking towards their traditional Milton End in the first half. Nigel Quashie swept over a great cross-field ball, which Matthew Taylor laid back into the path of Paul Merson. The Pompey captain flicked a pass over the top for Taylor, who charged into the box and buried a low shot into the left-hand corner: 1-0. But 6 minutes later, the Seagulls were level. With too much space given to Barrett, the ball broke to Brighton skipper Danny Cullip, who drilled a low shot into the Fratton End.

Quashie appealed for a penalty after being sent flying by Cullip in the box, only to be booked by over-zealous referee Bennett for diving. Richard Hughes then made matters worse on 19 minutes, with the ball at his feet 25 yards out from his own goal. He passed back to Hislop without looking, only for Brooker to nip in and tuck his shot past Pompey's 'keeper. The Seagulls had stunned the large crowd expecting a Pompey win with 2 goals in 10 minutes.

On 26 minutes, Guy Butters held down Deon Burton in the box and the yellow-shirted referee pointed to the spot. 3,000 Brighton fans behind the Milton goal booed incessantly as Merson stepped up and sent Petterson the wrong way with a low shot. The equaliser settled Pompey's nerves to create further good chances for Taylor, Quashie and Todorov. Petterson was by now having to keep the Seagulls in the game, until the last minute of the first half when Quashie, who had a splendid match, swept the ball across to Taylor, who in turn rolled in a perfect low cross which beat the ex-Pompey 'keeper at the near post to give Todorov a simple tap-in – with 5 goals in 45 minutes, Fratton Park was buzzing in an atmosphere of almost cup-tie proportions.

The best goal of the match came from Jason Crowe. One of only two players left in the team from the previous season, his confidence had visibly improved as a result of the Palace match. The former Arsenal full-back was fed a lovely pass from Merson, which travelled 40 yards down the right flank. Crowe steadied himself to curl a 25-yard shot into the top left-hand corner of the net to send the Fratton End into raptures. Pompey now had a full-back as joint top-scorer with 3!

Portsmouth 4
Taylor, Merson (penalty)
Todorov, Crowe

Brighton & Hove Albion 2
Cullip
Brooker

PORTSMOUTH *v.* BRIGHTON & HOVE ALBION

Harry Redknapp in typical pose, concentrating hard on what's going on.

Pompey's fifth win in 6 games provided the club's best start to any season since 1948. The only dampener on an exciting afternoon involved four more bookings – for Hughes, Foxe, Quashie and Taylor. Taylor escaped a red in a tangle on the ground with Barrett, who was sent off for Brighton in the closing minutes. The Pompey team were given a standing ovation on the final whistle with a chorus of 'We are top of the League' ringing around the ground.

Portsmouth: Hislop, Festa, De Zeeuw, Foxe, Crowe, Taylor, Quashie, Hughes, Merson, Todorov, Burton. Subs: Burchill, Harper, Robinson, Primus, Kawaguchi.
Brighton & Hove Albion: Petterson, Pethick, Watson, Cullip, Butters, Carpenter, Oatway, Melton, Marney, Brooker, Barrett. Subs: Packham, Rogers, Jones, Wilkinson, Hinshelwood.

TRUE GRIT

Date: Saturday 7 September 2002
Attendance: 8,797

Referee: Steven Baines (Chesterfield)
Man of the Match: Paul Merson/Arjan de Zeeuw

The old-fashioned open terrace holding 1,200 Pompey fans – their full allocation – in the run-down Kentish town of Gillingham summed up this match. An open and honest crash-barrier terrace, which held many memories of matches gone, was reached through a cul-de-sac road of terraced housing. It was another downbeat ground on the away day marathon for Pompey's travelling support, but a place of ambience.

Shocked by the sudden lack of Hayden Foxe (hamstring) and Deon Burton (foot), Pompey fans knew Gillingham were a stern side to face at home, although they had eight players out injured from their small squad of twenty-five. Pompey fielded replacements Linvoy Primus and Mark Burchill who were to show character and continue the winning habit.

Pompey were in control from the moment Paul Merson buried his third goal of the season from Matt Taylor's cross on the half-hour. The gold shirts could have been in front sooner, with Burchill and Merson going close, but both placed their shots just wide. The Gills had a spell of control but found Pompey's defence too composed with Primus, De Zeeuw and Festa showing a barrier of solidarity at the back. Quashie went close with a shot which flew narrowly wide of Bartram's post on a ground which on Boxing Day the previous season had seen one of Pompey's worst performances.

Unlike the Pompey of old, for the fourth time this season, another goal was scored just before half-time to double their lead. The Gills defence failed to deal with Merson's flick forward and Mark Burchill snapped it up, tucking in a low shot underneath Bartram for 2-0.

In the second half, Pompey continued the good work and were looking confident going forward, with Paul Merson continually opening up the Gills defence. However, shortly after Kevin Harper replaced Crowe down the right, the run of the game changed. On 68 minutes, Saunders swung in a deep cross, which Taylor lost to James, who calmly slotted the ball back across Hislop. A true test of character was the manner in which Pompey dealt with Gillingham's pressure, which they piled on with several raids. Shaw should have equalised when Ipoua beat three gold shirts, only to miss an open goal, and he missed another from just 3 yards out, with Harper kicking away the loose ball.

Gary O'Neil came on for the tiring Burchill and helped Pompey to round off a splendid afternoon's work 11 minutes from time. Merson stormed into the Gills half on a counter-attack, with Quashie and O'Neil breaking right and left. Pompey's skipper, who had a hand in all of the Pompey goals, released a delightful through-ball, which was perfectly timed for O'Neil to race through and stroke his shot casually past Bartram before racing off to celebrate in front of the Pompey fans: 3-1.

Gillingham 1
James

Portsmouth 3
Merson
Burchill
O'Neil

Pompey captain Paul Merson cannot hide his pleasure at opening the scoring against Gillingham.

All the talk coming out of the Priestfield Stadium from Pompey's noisy army of supporters was of having collected 3 away wins by the first week of September. Mine was of the referee, a former Chesterfield and Wrexham player, who smiled and understood the game throughout; an excellent official and a shining example to the rest of his colleagues.

Gillingham: Bartram, Edge, Patterson, Ashby, Hope, Smith, Shaw, Saunders, Hessenthaler, Johnson, Ipoua. Subs: Rose, Pennock, James, Awuah, Perpetuini.
Portsmouth: Hislop, Festa, De Zeeuw, Primus, Crowe, Taylor, Quashie, Hughes, Merson, Todorov, Burchill. Subs: Vincent, Harper, Cooper, O'Neil, Kawaguchi.

Date: Saturday 14 September 2002
Attendance: 17,201

Referee: Steven Tomlin (East Sussex)
Man of the Match: Gianluca Festa

A midweek Worthington Cup win over Peterborough United brought several injuries to Pompey's winning side and forced Harry Redknapp to make three changes. Vincent Pericard replaced Mark Burchill, who hurt his calf in the cup tie. Kevin Harper took the place of Jason Crowe and Carl Robinson filled in for Richard Hughes (hamstring).

Pompey had allowed 704 Millwall fans to buy tickets for a fixture traditionally fuelled with problems outside the ground and riot police were on hand to ensure there weren't any. The segregation at the Milton End between Pompey and Millwall fans had to be large, which reduced Pompey's overall attendance considerably, but with loanee Saint Kevin Davies and former Pompey favourite Steve Claridge warming up on the pitch for the Lions, the atmosphere was still full of spark.

Both teams fielded patched-up sides, and the first-half display illustrated a lack of consistency from both. The noon kick-off had perhaps unsettled the players. Pompey struggled to get going properly and, at times, found it difficult even to get out of their own half. The loudest cheers heard were from the Fratton End, who gave relentless stick to Kevin Davies for his sin of playing along the M27 west. Pericard burst down the right midway through the half and crossed for Merson, but the Pompey skipper's effort flew tamely wide.

Millwall looked the better side as frustration grew for those in Pompey's royal blue shirts, with loose balls being lost and a general lack of continuity among the squad. Claridge livened the game up in a duel with Arjan De Zeeuw, which ended in both players squaring up to each other after a challenge. Claridge was then booked for dissent beneath the South Stand for mouthing off to the linesman, and De Zeeuw was carded too.

The match grew into a bad-tempered affair, with Quashie and then Davies being cautioned, and Todorov then summed up the first 45 minutes by blazing a shot wide of the post when it seemed easier to score in the best chance of the match. A roasting from Harry and Jim at half-time clearly did the trick in waking up the team and pressing them into firm action. Just 5 minutes into the second half, Quashie slipped a magnificent pass through, which split the Lions defence, for Todorov to make amends for his earlier miss and race into the box and coolly lift his shot over Warner for his third goal of the season.

Pompey continued to pressurise the Millwall back three, forcing several corners; Merson, Quashie and Todorov all having chances which came to nothing. Quashie saved a potential equaliser at the other end by making an excellent tackle when Davies found the ball at his feet inside the box. Primus too cleared a header from Davies' cross to thwart Claridge. Todorov limped off to increase Pompey's injury concerns, Pompey re-grouped and O'Neil then curled a great effort from Merson just past the post.

Portsmouth 1	Millwall 0
Todorov	

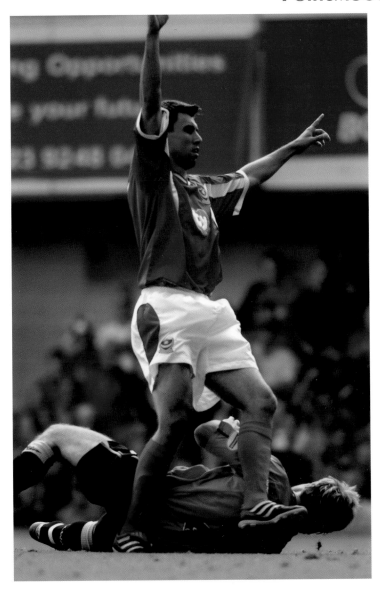

Bulgarian striker Svetoslav
Todorov acknowledges
the Fratton End applause
v. Millwall.

The final whistle was a great relief to both teams and their supporters as Pompey notched up their sixth straight win and seventh overall in 8 games. After the match, Millwall boss Mark McGhee soured the game by telling the waiting press: 'the division lacks quality if Portsmouth are leading it on this performance'. Those words were to haunt him six months later.

Portsmouth: Hislop, Festa, Primus, De Zeeuw, Harper, Taylor, Robinson, Quashie, Merson, Todorov, Pericard. Subs: Burchill, Tiler, O'Neil, Cooper, Kawaguchi.
Millwall: Warner, Lawrence, Bull, Nethercott, Ward, Livermore, Ifill, Kinet, Roberts, Davies, Claridge. Subs: Gueret, Ryan, Harris, Braniff, Phillips.

Date: Tuesday 17 September 2002
Attendance: 18,837

Referee: Paul Danson (Leicester)
Man of the Match: Matthew Taylor

Seldom are two successive games less alike, and happily so. As much as Saturday's win was dour to watch, an evening match under floodlights in late autumn, against a side who wanted to play football instead of just defend, was entertainment of the highest order. The attendance was swelled by Pompey's generous offer to seat adults on the Milton End for £15 with two children for £1 each. Homework was put aside and a dry forecast resulted in blue and white colours on all four sides of the old ground.

Wimbledon's home support had dropped recently to just 2,165, so it made sense to open up the Milton End to those who were not concerned about a move to Milton Keynes. Pompey lost the toss and kicked towards the old Goods Yard End first; but any superstitious worries were soon ended when Vincent Pericard chested Merson's pass before smashing his second goal of the season into the bottom corner of the net in just the 3rd minute.

It was all square 10 minutes later though, as Jason McAnuff – a torment against Pompey the previous season – escaped Taylor's reach to curl a far-post cross over to Neil Shipperley, who headed past Hislop. Game on. Matthew Taylor took the bull by the horns and, on 32 minutes, he showed why he is knocking on the door of the full England side. His turn of pace left Mark Williams standing. Merson found Taylor down the left with a precision pass, which Taylor latched onto, touching the ball around one red shirt before racing onto his own pass and sprinting like a Olympic athlete. His perfect cross matched the pace and Todorov buried a far-post header into the net. Cue the Fratton End to salute Pompey's young wing-back. The goal oozed class and the ground's populace were still discussing it minutes later.

On 39 minutes, Wimbledon defender Mark Williams knocked a pass back to his 'keeper Kelvin Davis who, to the delight of the teasing Fratton End, missed his kick completely, only to watch the ball trickle over the line! 3-1. Many Pompey fans missed the howler as they were waiting for the ball to land upfield from his kick. This repaid Wimbledon for the Alan Knight/Noel Blake comedy of 1984!

The second half proved just as entertaining a spectacle for supporters. The football flowed just as fast, and the Fratton End choir even found time to invite the other three sides of the ground to sing a song, which they did in turn. It was that sort of night. But for the eighteen Wimbledon fans perched at the very top of the Milton End north corner, their evening got worse. Williams was handed his second yellow card for a deliberate trip on Pericard, and he became the fifth visiting player in as many games at Fratton Park to take an early bath. Despite McAnuff keeping their faint hopes alive with his spirited runs, Pompey wrapped the night up with a deserved goal for Man of the Match Matthew Taylor. Once again, Merson the distributor released Taylor in the box and with precision – and no pausing – the

Portsmouth 4
Pericard, Todorov
M. Williams (own goal), Taylor

Wimbledon 1
Shipperley

Pompey's on-loan Frenchman Vincent Pericard in combat against Wimbledon.

England Under-21 star rammed in his second goal of the season off the far post, with 17 minutes left.

The laughter was not yet over. With Pompey winning 4-1, and different chants being sung from all four sides of the ground again, Paul Merson and referee Paul Danson ran into each other like circus characters, both collapsing in a heap to warrant both trainers running on to deliver treatment with their sponge and bucket. Half-a-dozen straight home wins, 7 straight League victories, 8 League and cup wins, 24 goals in 10 games, unbeaten and top of the League – this was the stuff dreams were made of. A club record of 7 successive wins in 1983 had also been equalled tonight.

Portsmouth: Hislop, Primus, Harper, Festa, De Zeeuw, Taylor, Robinson, Quashie, Merson, Todorov, Pericard. Subs: Burchill, O'Neil, Tiler, Vincent, Kawaguchi.
Wimbledon: Davis, Hawkins, Williams, McAnuff, Francis, Shipperley, Andersen, Nowland, Gier, Tapp, Darlington. Subs: Heald, Ainsworth, Wilmott, Gray, Leigertwood.

Pompey fans were still talking about Matt Taylor's pinpoint pass minutes after Todorov restored the lead against Wimbledon

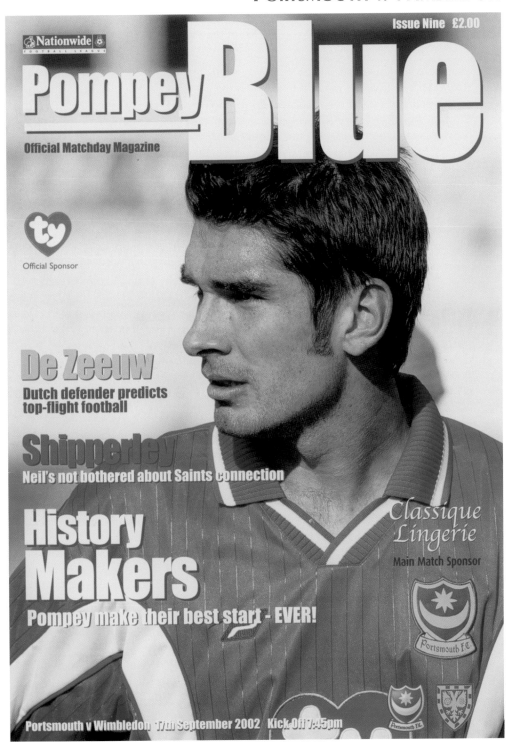

Pompey's match programme portrayed Under-21 Scottish international Richard Hughes, who was dogged by injury last season.

Date: Saturday 21 September 2002
Attendance: 21,335

Referee: Brian Curson (Leicestershire)
Man of the Match: Arjan De Zeeuw

League match number ten brought Pompey's first defeat. It was an awkward-looking fixture with Norwich – play-off final losers the previous season – favourites to go up this time and sitting in the top three. It was the match Pompey critics said would be the test. Manager Harry Redknapp decided to play just one striker in front of Paul Merson, with a trio midfield of Robinson, Quashie and O'Neil. A bright, warm, sunny day in Norfolk and a sell-out crowd greeted the teams as they trotted down the Carrow Road tunnel onto a fine pitch. A total of 2,143 Pompey fans greeted their unbeaten XI wearing traditional home colours of blue, white and red.

Todorov, playing alone, tried his best on several occasions, but the City defence got there first as Pompey lacked penetration and support up front. Norwich saw two shots go wide, but it was Pompey who had the edge when Matt Taylor won a corner. Merson laid the ball back to Quashie, whose 25-yard effort beat 'keeper Green but clipped the outside of the post. Norwich City's supporters were becoming restless as their chances were few and those they had were foiled by Hislop in the Pompey goal. Linvoy Primus, too, coped well in mopping up any City raids. The first half became a stalemate, with Pompey's overmanned midfield stifling the Canaries. Just before half-time, De Zeeuw was the Pompey hero as he nodded the ball away to safety from a Nedergaard header, which beat Hislop. This would have been an undeserved lead.

No substitutions were made by either side at half-time, and with Pompey on the back of 7 successive wins, they seemed content to continue plugging away with no serious attempt on goal. Midway through the second half, the game burst into life as Matthew Taylor charged through from box to box and released a left-foot strike, which Green had to save at the second attempt. At the other end, Carl Robinson kept out a dangerous cross from Holt, after the Norwich midfielder had broken clear and cut along the by-line. The large crowd now sensed a goal as the tempo increased, but it was Pompey who went nearest, with Merson forcing an excellent one-handed save from Green, after a Todorov and Harper move upfield. Pericard replaced Todorov on 72 minutes, shortly before Pompey should have taken the lead. Merson floated another corner onto De Zeeuw's head, but the defender was unlucky to see his effort loop over the bar with Green off his line and beaten.

With just 9 minutes left, the Canaries took an unjust lead from a corner, forced by Hislop turning Mulryne's 25-yard shot around the post. Nedergaard spun an inch-perfect cross for Iwan Roberts to jump in between De Zeeuw and Festa and head home. Harry Redknapp then swapped Robinson for Burchill to join Pericard up front with 7 minutes left and, in the dying minutes, Pompey nearly had a late equaliser when the Frenchman rounded Green in the goalmouth to lay a pass back for Burchill, whose shot was cut out by Mackay. The country's top-scorers had registered their first blank of the season and become the last side in the entire Nationwide League to lose a game, but they were still top of Division One by 2 points.

Norwich City 1
Roberts

Portsmouth 0

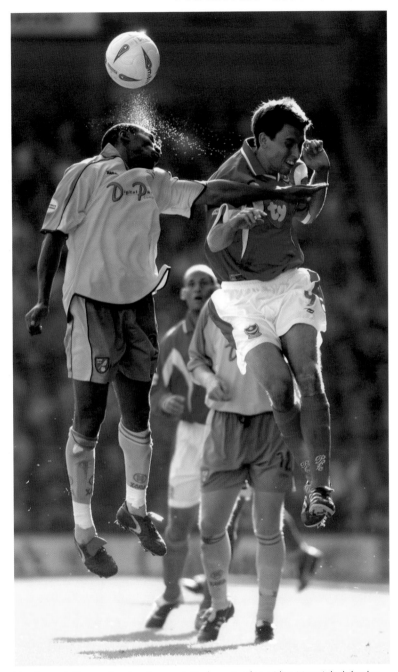

Heads up at Carrow Road as Pompey's Todorov tussles with a Norwich defender.

Norwich City: Green, Kenton, Mackay, Drury, Emblen, Holt, Mulryne, Nedergaard, Heckingbottom, McVeigh, Roberts. Subs: Crichton, Easton, Nielsen, Sutch, Llewellyn.
Portsmouth: Hislop, Festa, Primus, De Zeeuw, Harper, Taylor, Robinson, Quashie, O'Neil, Merson, Todorov. Subs: Pericard, Burchill, Ritchie, Cooper, Kawaguchi.

Date: Saturday 28 September 2002
Attendance: 18,459

Referee: Joe Ross (London)
Man of the Match: Paul Merson/Nigel Quashie

Another glorious sunny September day matched the warm feeling prevalent among most of the large crowd, who filed into all four sides of the ground due to the opposition's poor away following. Just 315 City fans travelled south, enabling Milton End tickets to be sold to Pompey fans, who basked in the autumn sunshine.

Pericard was the only change to Pompey's team, restoring his partnership with Todorov, Gary O'Neil returning to the bench. Former Pompey 'keeper, Dave Beasant, now forty-three, was on the bench for City. Pompey opened the game nervously, giving the ball away on several occasions to gift City some openings, but they all proved off-target. Against the run of play, on 17 minutes, Nigel Quashie netted his first goal of the season through a fine team move. Pericard chased a long ball down the right flank and touched the ball back to Harper, who squared it for Quashie to smash a low first-time left-footed shot in off Banks' left-hand post in the City goal. 1-0.

Just 4 minutes later, Pompey doubled their lead. Paul Merson and Matt Taylor swapped passes down the left before Merson launched the ball into the box for Pericard, who sprang the off-side trap, controlled the ball with his chest, and slammed in a low shot past Banks. It was his third goal of the season.

Several more chances fell to Pompey as the half wore on, with Pompey very much in the driving seat – Merson and Todorov had a couple of shots each, which were either saved or went wide. Early in the second half, City had their best chance of the game when Gus Uhlenbeek ran down the right and cut back to cross for Danny Cadamarteri to shoot at Hislop, who deflected his fierce strike over the bar. Bradford forced nine corners throughout the match and caused a few problems, but never looked like scoring with just the one shot on target from Cadamarteri.

On 58 minutes, the game was sewn up through a fine move by Paul Merson. Pericard won possession in his own half and passed to Merson, who charged through the City defence for Taylor and Quashie to run onto the same ball. Quashie reached it first and hammered his shot under Banks for his second of the match – 3-0. Apart from a momentary scare caused by Quashie, Festa and Robinson all needing treatment for injuries, the Pompey team kept the Bradford side at bay for another 3 points and another clean sheet – with 7 home wins on the bounce, the shirt-sleeved crowd went home happy. The League table after the game showed relegated Leicester City's home record to match Pompey's of '6-0-0', which provided great incentive for the month of October.

Portsmouth 3
Quashie (2)
Pericard

Bradford City 0

Paul Merson salutes a fine performance with satisfaction after helping Pericard to score Pompey's third goal.

Portsmouth: Hislop, Festa, Primus, De Zeeuw, Harper, Taylor, Robinson, Quashie, Merson, Todorov, Pericard. Subs: Burchill, O'Neil, Cooper, Ritchie, Kawaguchi.
Bradford City: Banks, Jacobs, Bower, Molenaar, Uhlenbeek, Evans, Jorgensen, Gray, Warnock, Proctor, Cadamarteri. Subs: Beasant, Juanjo, Standing, Emanuel, Reid.

FIVE-GOAL THRILLER

Date: Saturday 5 October 2002
Attendance: 8,604

Referee: Graham Laws (Whitley Bay)
Man of the Match: Shaka Hislop

With a midweek Worthington cup-tie defeat against Wimbledon behind them, it was important to concentrate on another away win at Rotherham. This was another of those matches that Pompey had lost the previous season, but they had to win now in order to keep up the pace. Hemmed in by scrapyards, cranes and railway lines, a ground like Millmoor is an intimidating place to visit. Rotherham were not the fall guys many had expected after their meteoric rise from Division Three.

Pompey's loud support numbered 1,509 under a roofed end dwarfed by giant cranes towering above the stand. This is a ground of homely, old-fashioned character – you step back in time to see an old cinema converted into a supporters' bar, three different stands of assorted height along one side of the ground, and children watching the game for free on the back wall of a pub.

Pompey fielded debutant Ivory Coast international Lassina Diabate, who had signed on a Bosman transfer during the week, and Paul Ritchie partnered Linvoy Primus in defence. A strange formation of 4-4-1-1 gradually became apparent as Nigel Quashie, back from an ankle injury, and with plenty of time and space, fired over the bar after 10 minutes. But on the quarter-hour, Vincent Pericard notched his third goal in a week as the Rotherham defenders failed to deal with a Taylor cross, and the Frenchman lapped up the loose ball at the far post to put it past the Millers 'keeper for 1-0.

The home side's response was an angry one, with defender Scott upending Taylor in spectacular fashion, which left the England Under-21 lad writhing in agony and brought assistant manager Jim Smith onto the pitch to argue with referee Laws. Taylor revealed a huge graze on his stomach, but Scott escaped even a caution. Millers' danger man Darren Byfield should have equalised on 22 minutes but made a dreadful miss, which stirred Pompey to increase their lead a minute later through Todorov's fifth goal of the season. Taylor was again the source, as he found Pericard with a deep cross, Pericard heading the ball back across the area for Toddy to tap in past 'keeper Pollitt: 2-0.

Against the run of play, the Millers clawed their way back into the game in the 34th minute, when Swailes swapped passes with Sedgwick before swinging in a cross for Byfield to nod in, despite Hislop getting a hand to it. Rotherham showed much spirit to bring the game level, but De Zeeuw, with Festa, had a fine game at the back to clear any possible danger. However, controversy reigned just before half-time which resulted in Pompey scoring in the 'lucky' 45th minute again. Todorov chased a ball through into the box when he was brought down by Swailes, whose contact seemed minimal. The referee pointed to the spot and then sent Swailes off to bring deafening abuse from the home fans. Merson ignored the chants, calmly slotting home a clean penalty, and he then took a majestic bow to incense the Tivoli End even more. The half-time whistle blew, 3-1.

Rotherham United 2
Byfield
Lee

Portsmouth 3
Pericard, Todorov
Merson (penalty)

Pompey 'keeper Shaka Hislop prevented Rotherham from equalising in the last minute with a fingertip save.

As so often happens in football, rather than working to Pompey's advantage, playing against ten men lifted the other side. With nothing to lose, the Millers piled forward and Hislop, De Zeeuw, Primus and Festa were kept busy. But then referee Laws – who was fast becoming the centre of attention by issuing eight yellow cards and one red – awarded what he saw as a penalty, although no Millers player appealed. Festa bumped into Lee as another Millers ball was hurled into the Pompey box. Lee sent Hislop the wrong way and now it was the Pompey supporters housed in the Railway End who hurled their anger at the official.

Pompey hung on and nearly scored a fourth, when Taylor's header struck a post from Paul Merson's cross, but the saving grace of the afternoon was a terrific fingertip save from Hislop in the last minute as Paul Hurst's 25-yard dipper was pushed onto the bar by the Pompey 'keeper and away for a corner. It was just a shame there were not more in the ground to see it.

Rotherham United: Pollitt, Scott, Swailes, McIntosh, Hurst, Sedgwick, Garner, Daws, Warne, Byfield, Barker. Subs: Mullin, Monkhouse, Lee, Gray, Robins.
Portsmouth: Hislop, Primus, De Zeeuw, Festa, Taylor, Ritchie, Pericard, Diabate, Quashie, Todorov, Merson. Subs: Robinson, Burchill, O'Neil, Harper, Kawaguchi.

Date: Saturday 18 October 2002   **Referee:** David Crick (Surrey)
Attendance: 18,837   **Man of the Match:** Gianluca Festa

With Wolves postponing the game planned for 12 October at short notice due to international call-ups, Pompey had a whole fortnight to rest and look back on their first dozen games' work with pride. Very few had expected to see Pompey top of the League in mid-October. 2,000 more season ticket sales in the match-less fortnight increased the total to 10,800, and Pompey started this game with confidence, having chalked up 4 away wins, equalling their total for the whole of the previous season.

Former 1948/49 Championship full-back Harry Ferrier had died in the week, aged eighty-two, and forty former Pompey players, back in the city for their bi-annual reunion, lined the tunnel for a minute's silence. It was another dry and sunny day, and the Fratton turf looked resplendent before another sell-out crowd. Coventry City wore an all-yellow strip and fielded former Pompey forward Lee Mills alone up front with a youthful side behind him, save for their player-manager Gary McAllister, aged thirty-eight.

Pompey opened the game up brightly, with Matt Taylor the architect as he fed Todorov with a fine pass in the opening minutes, but the Bulgarian's shot sped past the post, and Diabate's effort, on his home debut, was fired over from another Taylor cross. Harry Redknapp had only made one change – swapping O'Neil in for Ritchie from the last match – and a reshuffle during the first half was necessary in Pompey's midfield as they had failed to break through against the tight marking from the Sky Blues.

Shortly before half-time, Todorov missed the best chance of the match as he hooked a shot from just 12 yards out over the bar. Lee Mills had several chances to take the lead for the visitors, hitting the bar twice to enhance Coventry's bid to be the best side to visit Fratton Park this season. The second half provided good entertainment for the crowd, with Gary McAllister enjoying a solid 45 minutes. His astute reading of the game, direction, vision and understanding with his players provided the stiffest test Pompey had endured so far.

But it was Pompey who took the lead on 51 minutes. During a rare moment when Coventry were exposed at the back, Merson fed Pericard to run through on goal, and the Frenchman then produced a delightful chip over the stranded Sky Blues 'keeper, Debec, for his sixth goal of the season. The goal changed Coventry's system and they brought on top scorer Gary McSheffrey to partner Lee Mills – within 9 minutes, City were level. A cross from Partridge caused confusion in Pompey's penalty area and took two ricochets before hitting Sky Blue's centre-half Davenport, who dribbled the ball over the line past wrong-footed Shaka Hislop.

City reverted to Mills up front on his own again to defend their goal, and it was Pompey who missed two golden chances with 15 minutes left. Unmarked at 15 yards out, Todorov chested the ball down and then fired over the Fratton End bar.

Portsmouth 1	Coventry City 1
Pericard	*Davenport*

It's mine. Former Pompey striker Lee Mills tries to hold off Arjan de Zeeuw.

Later, De Zeeuw saw his header crash off the bar too. However, in the last few minutes, Pompey nearly lost the game, which could have gone either way with the chances scorned by both sides, as Partridge missed a close-range effort which hit Hislop's leg. A draw was a fair result, ending Pompey's 100 per cent record at home.

Portsmouth: Hislop, Festa, De Zeeuw, Primus, Taylor, O'Neil, Diabate, Quashie, Merson, Todorov, Pericard. Subs: Harper, Burchill, Robinson, Ritchie, Kawaguchi.
Coventry City: Debec, Davenport, Konjic, Caldwell, Quinn, Safri, McAllister, Pipe, Chippo, Partridge, Mills. Subs: Gordon, Eustace, McSheffrey, Bothroyd, Hyldgaard.

Date: Saturday 26 October 2002   **Referee:** Mark Clattenburg (Chester-le-Street)
Attendance: 15,788   **Man of the Match:** Steve Stone

Turf Moor in East Lancashire is a ground at which Pompey teams of previous decades have struggled to achieve a win bonus. Both pre- and post-war, a Pompey XI could not strike a winning formula in the town once renowned for its chimneys. An eight-hour coach journey up the M6 the day before the match was hardly positive preparation either, forcing Saturday morning training instead of the planned Friday afternoon session at Blackburn. This was a first for Paul Merson, who in sixteen years as a footballer had never trained on the morning of a match.

Pompey's loyal away support of 1,206 also had problems on the Saturday – many of them missed the first half of the match with delays on the M40 and the infamous M6 between the Midlands and Manchester. Those who were there at kick-off saw a loanee from Aston Villa make his Pompey debut – former England international Steve Stone. Harry Redknapp formed an attacking line-up with Todorov and Pericard up front, and Paul Ritchie deputised in defence for Festa, who was ruled out with a knee injury.

Pompey tore into the Clarets right from the start, showing no signs of their re-arranged training schedule. Todorov, Taylor and Pericard all linked well for two early moves, which Burnley 'keeper Marlon Beresford saved well. On 20 minutes, Pompey took a deserved lead following a move started by debutant Steve Stone. He fed Todorov down the right, whilst Pericard made a run through the middle. Todorov accurately squared for Quashie, who took a few seconds to balance himself before burying a low, angled shot into the right-hand corner of the net, in front of Pompey's adoring fans.1-0.

Stone himself found the net a few minutes later from a low cross by Taylor, but his effort was declared off-side. Beresford then had to smother two further Pompey attacks, both started by Stone, who was showing his Premiership talent and thirst for the game, having not played for some time. After the break, Pompey continued to impress with their quality, width and strength against a side tipped for the play-offs, who were unbeaten in 12 games. In the 58th minute, Taylor fed Todorov with a cross and the Bulgarian jinked and weaved his way cleverly round several claret-and-blue shirts, before releasing a shot which looked as though Beresford had covered, but the ball bobbled over the 'keeper and into the net for 2-0.

Bookings for Diabate, Ritchie, Taylor and Merson did not detract from a magnificent Pompey performance, as Burnley even missed a penalty (Dean West hit the bar) after Briscoe's low cross smacked Stone's arm. Pompey had nine shots on target in the match, which included a third goal scored 4 minutes from time. Substitute Kevin Harper received a perfect cross from Stone to volley home at the far post. Burnley were shell-shocked, and even allowed substitute Carl Robinson to have a shot cleared off the line, and Paul Ritchie saw a header bounce off the post to prevent a 0-5 scoreline. Pompey had been in total control for their fifth away win

---

Burnley 0   Portsmouth 3
Quashie, Todorov
Harper

Nigel Quashie, Matt Taylor and Todorov celebrate behind Burnley's goal.

of the season – as many as they normally get in a whole season – and Steve Stone had fitted into the Pompey jigsaw perfectly.

The only downsides of the day were the picky referee, Burnley's usual partisan and unfriendly support and the biased tannoy-man, who would not announce any of Pompey's goalscorers. However, outweighing those negatives was a stunning Pompey performance, which gave the club a 6-point lead at the top of the Division One table.

Burnley: Beresford, West, Cox, Gnohere, Branch, Little, Davis, Briscoe, Moore, G. Taylor, Blake.
    Subs: Papadopoulous, Maylott, Weller, Cook, Grant.
Portsmouth: Hislop, Primus, De Zeeuw, Ritchie, Taylor, Diabate, Quashie, Stone, Merson, Todorov, Pericard. Subs: Harper, Robinson, O'Neil, Burchill, Kawaguchi.

Date: Tuesday 29 October 2003   **Referee:** Paul Armstrong (Berkshire)
Attendance: 18,637   **Man of the Match:** Arjan De Zeeuw

On his first visit to Hampshire, former Scotland manager Craig Brown showed himself up with one of those press quotes he must have wished he'd never said. Trying to impress with his knowledge of Pompey's 14 matches so far, he publicly enquired how Pompey would cope if they fell a goal behind to his Preston side with one away defeat. Pompey obliged by going a goal down, but then rattled in 3 goals in 11 minutes to answer his question!

On a perfect floodlit October evening, with a delayed kick-off due to an accident on the M275, the first half was as exhausting to watch for spectators as it was for the players whose energy went into overdrive. It was one of those first halves many fans wished they could bottle up and take home with them to keep. Preston midfielder Graham Alexander had his fierce shot parried by Pompey 'keeper Shaka Hislop, only for Cresswell to react first and nod in the rebound for 1-0. Craig Brown smiled as his Lancashire side continued to stifle Pompey's midfield until Steve Stone intelligently found a way through, showing Pompey's home fans his pedigree.

Lacking a Fratton Park goal by anyone against Preston since 1982, Stone nudged in Matt Taylor's low cross on 23 minutes to bring an equaliser. Another 2 minutes later, the referee provided the turning point in awarding a fortuitous penalty, when Pericard appeared to slip rather than fall after contact with Rob Edward's foot. Merson stepped up to the Milton End to hit his fifth of the season low into the corner – 2-1. Pompey dominated with vigour, as Quashie twice went close with shots that went narrowly past the post in a rampant 10-minute spell.

On 34 minutes, Matt Taylor had the crowd out of their seats with an overlapping run of electrifying pace from which he then delivered, without pausing, a perfect lob over the advancing Preston 'keeper to make it 3-1. But Preston counter-attacked, and missing Linvoy Primus, who had been dropped for the return of Festa, Cresswell broke through, beat Hislop from outside the box only to see his shot bounce back off the post. American international Eddie Lewis curled a 25-yard shot wide. It was that sort of half.

After a breathtaking first half, the second was laboured, save for Ritchie being penalised for bringing down Rankine just 40 seconds after the restart. Alexander scored from the spot, as he had done the previous season against Pompey, to reduce the arrears and the Fratton crowd looked for a tense game. Instead, both teams chose to defend stoutly, particularly Pompey, to protect 7 home wins from 8. De Zeeuw, Festa and Ritchie were a credit to Pompey's defence as they mopped up any Preston breakthroughs, and the visitors failed to create any serious chances.

After the match, with Pompey now 7 points clear at the top, Craig Brown redeemed his earlier comment by suggesting that his side had been beaten by the eventual title winners come the end of the season.

Portsmouth 3
Stone, Merson (penalty)
Taylor

Preston North End 2
Cresswell
Alexander (penalty)

Steve Stone, another of Harry Redknapp's inspired signings during the season.

Portsmouth: Hislop, Festa, De Zeeuw, Ritchie, Stone, Diabate, Quashie, Taylor, Merson, Pericard, Todorov. Subs: O'Neil, Harper, Primus, Burchill, Kawaguchi.
Preston North End: Lucas, Lucketti, Broomes, Murdock, Alexander, Edwards, McKenna, Rankine, Skora, Lewis, Cresswell. Subs: Abott, Etuhu, Jackson, Healy, Moilanen.

TOTAL FARCE

Date: Saturday 2 November 2002
Attendance: 19,107

Referee: Andrew Hall (Birmingham)
Man of the Match: Linvoy Primus

In a much-awaited fixture between the top two sides, which should have been a great advertisement for Division One, only the referee knew why he allowed the game to start. The conditions – farcical at 1.30 p.m. and totally unplayable by 3.30 p.m. – ruined any entertainment as a football match for Pompey's largest crowd of the season. It was water polo at best. Not a single pass could be made.

With a weather forecast of heavy rain throughout the afternoon, referee Andrew Hall defied belief in allowing the game to go ahead, with puddles on the pitch before kick-off that soon became 100 yards of water down both flanks by 3.30 p.m. No one would have complained if he had postponed the match just before kick-off. Proper football was impossible and the crowd were effectively cheated of their entrance money. Players skidded all over the pitch and spectators sitting in the front rows of seats shied away when tackles neared to avoid another soaking.

The referee ruined a sell-out crowd atmosphere by allowing the game to continue and, even worse, the monsoon conditions lead to a casualty in Gianluca Festa. Pompey's Italian defender slid 10 yards off the pitch into a water carrier and sustained a serious knee injury. Leicester City, to their credit, adapted to the conditions better than Pompey, who could not play their usual passing style of football. Pompey, as the team from the home of the Royal Navy, did not enjoy the ocean wave, whereas the East Midland landlubbers proved more seaworthy!

The Foxes took the lead on 13 minutes, when Paul Dickov squirmed down the left and cut a cross back for Scowcroft to swivel and beat Hislop from close range. The former Premiership side sealed their watery win 6 minutes before half-time, when Matt Elliott glanced in a near-post header beyond Hislop from a corner. Pompey's home record was dented for the first time, but the real loser was football and the paying spectators. The rain was incessant and if anything fell harder as the second half progressed.

After the match, Paul Merson revealed on BBC Radio Solent that the referee had told him at 1-0 during the game that if Pompey equalised, he would abandon the match, which only served to rub salt into Pompey's damp wounds. No football match at Fratton Park had been stopped since January 1955, and no one would have complained if this had been the next. Long faces drooped hours after the 'game' had finished and the non-event will still be talked about for years to come as the worst conditions witnessed in living memory.

Days after the charade, the Pompey chairman branded the referee 'totally irresponsible' and filed an official complaint to the Football Association, which, as always, fell on deaf ears. Leicester manager Micky Adams was more concerned with the money crisis his club were suffering off the field, with his entire squad taking a 15 per cent paycut to help ease their financial situation whilst in administration.

Portsmouth 0

Leicester City 2
Scowcroft
Elliott

Matt Taylor takes an early shower on the pitch.

Portsmouth: Hislop, Primus, Festa, De Zeeuw, Stone, Diabate, Merson, Quashie, Taylor, Todorov, Pericard. Subs: Ritchie, O'Neil, Burchill, Harper, Kawaguchi.

Leicester City: Walker, Sinclair, Elliott, Taggart, Davidson, Scowcroft, McKinlay, Izzet, Rogers, Dickov, Deane. Subs: Impey, Benjamin, Stewart, Stevenson, Summerbee.

Date: Wednesday 6 November 2002   **Referee:** Graham Salisbury (Preston)
Attendance: 27,022   **Man of the Match:** Paul Ritchie

The two longest-serving members of Division One provided a good spectacle of entertainment for a large crowd in this rearranged floodlit match. Keen to play some football away from the sodden south of England, a farce of another kind led to the Pompey squad not arriving at the magnificent rebuilt stadium until 40 minutes before kick-off. The team coach broke down between the hotel and the ground, forcing players and directors to use their own cars to travel, but despite hurried preparations, they showed no ill effects as a result of their late and unusual arrival.

Pompey revealed to the partisan Wolves audience why they led the table. Throughout the 90 minutes of this fiercely contested game, which ended with two Wolves strikers taken to hospital for X-rays, Pompey, playing in their third all-white strip, passed the ball around with commendable control and possession. Ritchie's tackle on Blake was perfectly timed from behind, but already weakened from a 4-0 away win at Gillingham, Blake's ankle gave in and he was stretchered off to Wolverhampton General after just 15 minutes. Diabate thundered into George Ndah on 33 minutes, with a two-footed sliding tackle which seemed worthy of a red card, and despite another trip for the stretcher-bearers, the Ivory Coast midfielder escaped with a yellow.

The crowd booed every Pompey move and pilloried the referee, which slightly marred an otherwise outstanding match of inter-passing football as good as you would see in the Premier League. Pompey played bright, open football to shake off the hangover of their first home defeat against Leicester, and when Quashie thumped an upright from 25 yards after a slick corner routine, it was a question of when, not if, Pompey would score the first goal.

Primus and Ritchie were outstanding in defence, with Steve Stone slotting into the right-back position to cover for the injured De Zeeuw. On 56 minutes, the threatened goal came with a delightful free-kick from Paul Merson. Quashie's run had been halted unfairly by Edworthy and Cooper 20 yards out, and Merson swung the ball up over the defensive wall and past Wolves 'keeper Murray, who didn't move.

A move of similar individual brilliance prevented Pompey from collecting their sixth away win just 6 minutes later. Dean Sturridge bustled his way through Pompey's defence and rifled a shot past Hislop to equalise. Both sides continued to search for a winner, with Hislop pulling off three good saves, including tipping over a header from Mark Clyde towards the end. The end result was a fair one and extended Pompey's lead to 5 points.

Wolverhampton Wanderers 1	Portsmouth 1
Sturridge	*Merson*

Wolves' scorer Dean Sturridge shields the ball from Pompey midfielder Lassina Diabate.

Wolverhampton Wanderers: Murray, Edworthy, Lescott, Clyde, Irwin, Rae, Ince, Cooper, Ndah, Blake, Miller. Subs: Sturridge, Kennedy, Newton, Oakes, Ingimarsson.
Portsmouth: Hislop, Primus, Taylor, Ritchie, Stone, Diabate, Quashie, Robinson, Merson, Todorov, Pericard. Subs: Harper, Burchill, O'Neil, Cooper, Kawaguchi.

Date: Saturday 9 November 2002
Attendance: 26,587

Referee: Howard Webb (Rotherham)
Man of the Match: Nigel Quashie/Arjan De Zeeuw

Derby, down from the Premier League, were something of an unknown quantity, apart from Pompey assistant manager Jim Smith's knowledge from his lengthy term of office there. The appeal of the unknown appeared strong enough to entice 3,792 Pompey fans to travel to the East Midlands to visit Derby's gargantuan Pride Park stadium, with its spaceship gantry outside and massive dome inside. Pompey's extraordinary support certainly struck a chord; the match and result equalled the superb away following.

Following a minute's silence for former Derby County captain and Pompey midfielder Rob Hindmarch, who had died at the age of forty-one after suffering from motor neurone disease, the Rams tore into Pompey from the start, giving the match the excitement the build-up deserved. De Zeeuw was back in a reshuffled defence, and Mark Burchill returned in place of Pericard. The Derby bench boasted Ravanelli and former Pompey favourite Deon Burton.

Georgi Kinkladze threatened early, with two chances scorned, and when Lee Morris wriggled into the box and was grounded by Diabate, a 16th-minute penalty was awarded and converted by Danny Higginbotham. Derby boss and former Pompey manager John Gregory appeared to have his team fired up to record their third straight win, but it was not to be. Nigel Quashie was having one of his better games, and it took a second grab from Derby 'keeper Lee Grant to keep out a fierce Quashie shot.

One of several improved qualities to enjoy as a Pompey spectator this season was the speed in which Pompey responded to going a goal down, not seen in many previous seasons. This match provided a fine example. On 27 minutes, Todorov released Burchill, who ran forward and spread the ball out to Taylor. He crossed first time for Toddy, who continued his run to sidefoot the ball into the corner of the net for his seventh of the season – 1-1.

After the interval, Hayden Foxe returned for his first taste of action since August to replace Ritchie, who had enjoyed a good first half. On 51 minutes, Pompey were ahead – a lead which had threatened to happen in a game made entertaining by both sides. Paul Merson burst out of his own half, fed Taylor down the left, who provided Burchill with the chance to rise above his opponents to head home a perfect cross. Burchill celebrated his third goal of the season in front of Pompey's massive support.

Derby became overwhelmed by Pompey's raiding attacks as they sought a third goal. The introduction of Ravanelli and Burton failed to stem the tide, as Todorov had a goal disallowed and a Rob Lee lunge at Merson, which blatantly should have produced a penalty, was turned down by referee Webb. Indeed, the poise and precision from Pompey's second-half performance overshadowed Derby and, but for Webb's decisions, Pompey could have won 4-1. Pompey captain Merson

---

Derby County 1
Higginbotham (penalty)

Portsmouth 2
Todorov
Burchill

It's in there. Captain Paul Merson (wearing gloves) celebrates Mark Burchill's goal to take the lead at Derby.

finished the game with a gashed Achilles – evidence of the turned-down penalty appeal.

On the final whistle, manager Harry Redknapp sent the whole Pompey team down to the cheering thousands of Pompey supporters, whose vocal support during the game had never ceased. He, too, in a rare moment of emotion, ran down the touchline and punched the air with delight. The Burnley win had been classy, but this was even better. By now, the nation's media were starting to take notice of the surprise team at the top of Division One with 42 points. Relegated Derby had only 24 points, while much-fancied Ipswich Town were struggling on 17 and lying fifth from bottom. Pompey, meanwhile, were, in total reverse of their normal away form, the best side in the country, having collected 20 points on their travels.

Derby County: Grant, Barton, Evatt, Higginbotham, Hunt, Bolder, Lee, Boertien, Kinkladze, McLeod, Morris. Subs: Riggott, Ravanelli, Burton, Twigg, Oakes.

Portsmouth: Hislop, Primus, De Zeeuw, Ritchie, Stone, Merson, Diabate, Quashie, Taylor, Todorov, Burchill. Subs: Foxe, Pericard, Harper, Robinson, Kawaguchi.

BULGARIAN DELIGHT

Date: Saturday 16 November 2002
Attendance: 18,701

Referee: Paul Taylor (Cheshunt)
Man of the Match: Svetoslav Todorov

Another former Pompey manager faced the onslaught of the table-topping Blues, as Tony Pulis brought an inherited Stoke side, promoted from Division Two, to an autumnal Fratton Park. Kevin Harper and Hayden Foxe replaced Paul Ritchie (torn stomach muscles) and Steve Stone (hamstring) and, uncharacteristically, Pompey gave the ball away on seven occasions in the first quarter of an hour.

Stoke, on the back of 6 straight defeats, looked equally unimpressive, and the first half became dull fare for the large crowd, who, in turn, became impatient. As so often with 'home bankers', Pompey's home support and the players appeared to give the impression that their mere attendance was enough for a win. This was summed up by the Fratton End singing odd songs in between strange periods of quietness, and the rare journey of Harry Redknapp from his traditional directors' box seat down to the dugout 5 minutes before half-time. The first 45 minutes were largely forgettable.

Fresh from a rollicking in the home dressing room, the Pompey team emerged in the second half to switch from a wing-back system to a back four to outweigh Stoke City's midfield. Matthew Taylor, who dropped back to play at full-back, still got away down the left and tested 'keeper Cutler with a low cross, which he kept out. But, on 49 minutes, Pompey were ahead. Harper got away down the right and delivered a perfect low cross which fellow Scotsman Mark Burchill met at the near-post and delivered with a firm right-footed drive high into the net – 1-0.

Todorov, who had tried hard in vain in the first half, went close with several chances, one of which was a first-time effort crashed off the bar from a Burchill pass. But, with Burchill tiring, Pericard replaced him as Pompey looked to increase their narrow lead. Pompey stepped up the urgency as Stoke struggled to find an equaliser. Quashie sailed a long-range effort into the Fratton End, Harper flew a shot just past the post, but with 3 minutes left, relief could be seen and heard around the ground as Todorov crossed at the Fratton End for Pericard to head home at the far post.

Those supporters foolish enough to leave before the end came running back when Pompey netted a third in injury-time, and the most deserving man on the pitch scored it. Watched by the Bulgarian national manager, Todorov's hard graft paid off as he received a delightful Merson flick-up over the Stoke defence to lob the advancing 'keeper for his eighth of the season.

Stoke proved, in typical Pulis style, a hard team to break down, but through the persistence of Harper and Todorov, Pompey unlocked the Stoke City back six to gain their eighth home win of an incredible season and stretch their lead over second-placed Leicester City to 7 points. Todorov, meanwhile, was showing his initial rusty start the previous March was in the past, his clever, crafty, hard-working and skilful play in tight spaces paying off to earn a deserved midweek trip to Spain with the Bulgarian national squad.

Portsmouth 3
Burchill, Pericard
Todorov

Stoke City 0

Leading goalscorer Svetoslav Todorov grafted hard against Stoke City to earn a late goal.

Portsmouth: Hislop, Primus, De Zeeuw, Foxe, Harper, Diabate, Quashie, Taylor, Merson, Todorov, Burchill. Subs: Pericard, Crowe, O'Neil, Robinson, Kawaguchi.

Stoke City: Cutler, Henry, Thomas, Handyside, Clarke, Hoekstra, Gunnarsson, Marteinsson, Gudjonsson, O'Connor, Mooney. Subs: Greenacre, Iwelumo, Vandeurzen, Viander, Cooke.

REACH FOR THE SKY

Date: Saturday 23 November 2002   **Referee:** Paul Danson (Leicestershire)
Attendance: 16,601   **Man of the Match:** Gary O'Neil/Svetoslav Todorov

Pompey and live television cameras have never been soulmates. Especially those cameras from Sky. With the famous old Yorkshire club residing in the bottom three and having acquired a new manager, lifelong supporter and former goalkeeper Chris Turner, Sheffield Wednesday v. Portsmouth was an odd game to broadcast at 5.35 p.m. on a November Saturday teatime, but since when do the decision-makers of satellite television base their choices in logic and reason? Pompey's first televised showing in their impressive season was a chance to show the football nation why they were top and to settle any doubters. Leicester had already won that day, and 1,235 Pompey fans behind the Leppings Lane goal were in full voice, with a massive flag being passed over their heads to show the viewing public that their southern support was as good as the team.

After Chris Turner had been introduced to the home crowd – the lowest of the season – Pompey kicked off in their familiar gold away strip against the Owls, who had lost 4 of the last 5 matches at home. Quashie's suspension and Stone's hamstring injury gave Carl Robinson and Vincent Pericard first-team chances, but it was Todorov who opened the scoring after 11 minutes. Pericard worked the ball out to Taylor, whose cross was punched out from under the bar by Owls 'keeper Pressman, after taking a deflection from one of his own defenders. The ball looped up and, although Beswetherick headed off the line, the ball came back down again for Todorov, who steadied himself coolly and half-volleyed into the corner of the net for 1-0.

Two tackles by Craig Armstrong then robbed Paul Merson of any further participation in the game, the second cruel challenge, which left the former England player clutching his right ankle, going unpunished by referee Danson. Replaced by Gary O'Neil in the 24th minute, the question for every Pompey follower was how would we cope without him? The answer was provided quickly, as Wednesday equalised within 2 minutes. Pressman's long punt forward was missed by Pompey's midfield and flicked on by Owusu to Knight, who nipped in and clipped the ball over a diving Hislop: 1-1.

It was Pompey who then started to become physical, Diabate and De Zeeuw both collecting yellow cards. But the Blues regained their earlier composure, and O'Neil, Todorov and Harper created several problems to worry Chris Turner in the home dugout. And worried he was, early in the second half, when a bizarre incident should have placed Pompey 2-1 up. O'Neil sent a superb ball through to Taylor, who crossed for Todorov to head in from 3 yards, but Pericard unfortunately got in the way and blocked his own team-mate's shot!

But, a minute later, the lead was restored. O'Neil found Pericard, who slipped Todorov through on goal. Todorov then sent Pressman the wrong way with a side-footed shot into the corner for his tenth goal of the season. Although Primus went

---

Sheffield Wednesday 1
Knight

Portsmouth 3
Todorov (2)
O'Neil

Substitute Gary O'Neil played a magnificent game at Hillsborough.

down with a groin injury and was replaced by Crowe, Pompey ruled the match and underlined their domination midway through the second half. On 64 minutes, Todorov was involved again, chasing the ball into a corner to cut a cross in for Pericard to beat Pressman with a simple tap-in, but he unselfishly squared the ball to O'Neil, who swept in to round off a creative performance as an England Under-20 captain replacing his senior former England colleague: 3-1.

Pressman saved another shot from Taylor in injury time to prevent a fourth goal, which would have been fully deserved, such was Pompey's dominance against a poor Owls side, who failed to provide one single chance in the second half. Pompey supporters gave the team a standing ovation at the end, and stood staring in disbelief at their team's first-ever win on Sky television and their seventh away win of the season. '48 points', one fan said to me as we filed out, 'why, we're almost safe!'.

Sheffield Wednesday: Pressman, Crane, Haslam, Bromby, Geary, Armstrong, Sibon, Quinn, Beswetherick, Knight, Owusu. Subs: Hamshaw, Donnelly, Morrison, Hendon, Stringer.
Portsmouth: Hislop, Primus, De Zeeuw, Foxe, Harper, Diabate, Robinson, Taylor, Merson, Todorov, Pericard. Subs: O'Neil, Crowe, Burchill, Pitt, Kawaguchi.

POMPEY 3 THE REFEREE 2

Date: Saturday 30 November 2002
Attendance: 17,701

Referee: Grant Hegley (Bishop's Stortford)
Man of the Match: Svetoslav Todorov

With another 1,200 season tickets sold in the week, Pompey's seated regulars numbered 12,000 – another record broken. Having lost just twice in 20 games, the Portsmouth public warmed to the fact that it was going to be a very interesting winter at Fratton Park, and many wanted to be part of the matchday audience. Unprecedented queues at the ticket office in Frogmore Road every day of the week were coped with by industrious club staff; interest in the local football team had not been this high since the FA Cup semi-final against Liverpool in April 1992.

Walsall arrived with plenty of warnings that their humble League position belied their ability, and by the 10th minute of an overcast match, that assessment rang true. While their team coach had needed to be pulled out of a muddy ditch in the club car park by a Pompey fan, the Walsall players showed no such lethargy. The Saddlers won two corners and Brazilian striker Junior curled a 30-yard free-kick against the Fratton End crossbar. Portuguese forward Jorge Leitao then forced Hislop to dive right to prevent another 30-yard shot from going in. Walsall manager Colin Lee had done his homework watching Pompey at Hillsborough.

It is no secret the vocal Fratton End support take no prisoners in dishing out their feelings to visiting players or officials; this has been witnessed for generations. But for all four sides of the ground and both managers to vent their frustration at the man in black, almost warranted an FA enquiry. Step forward Mr Grant Hegley for having a bad afternoon. In the 31st minute, Diabate gave the ball away to Junior in his own half, who slipped a fine ball through to Corica who was 'pushed' by Ritchie from behind in the Fratton penalty box. 'Penalty' said Hegley, 1-0 to Walsall. Quashie, Ritchie, Sonner and Wrack then entered his notebook, as Hegley turned the game into a bad-tempered affair before Pompey grabbed an equaliser in first-half injury-time. Harper's excellent cross was only half-cleared for Nigel Quashie to volley in his fifth of the season to make it 1-1.

The second half was as lively as the first, with Merson creating some fine breaks for Pompey, which led to Pericard and Todorov testing Walker. On 58 minutes, Pompey took the lead from a corner taken by Merson to Pericard, who then returned the ball to Merson to lightly curl the ball in for Todorov, who headed into the corner beyond Walker for his eleventh of the campaign – 2-1. Pompey fans immediately burst into song at the prospect of breaking the 50-point barrier: 'We're not going down'. But the happy mood changed again when the referee handed another controversial penalty to Walsall on 68 minutes. Sonner appeared to throw himself theatrically to the ground under Crowe's influence. To everyone's surprise, Hegley pointed to the spot and Sonner stepped up to send Hislop the wrong way to make it 2-2.

Taylor and Leitao then received yellow cards, before Kevin Harper was sent sprawling in an off-the-ball incident. Tempers flared, with sixteen players pushing

---

Portsmouth 3
Quashie, Todorov
Taylor

Walsall 2
Sonner (2 penalties)

'What's going on, ref?' Paul Merson is as astonished with Mr Hegley as the Pompey fans are.

and shoving in the Pompey box. Anticipating yellow or red cards, the whole crowd was left aghast as Hegley discussed the brawl with both his assistants and booked … no one. With 14 minutes left, Fratton Park erupted at the end of an explosive afternoon, when Matthew Taylor restored Pompey's lead. Todorov won possession by the corner flag and cut a cross back for Quashie, whose shot was saved with Pericard's follow-up effort blocked. But, as the ball spun out to Taylor, he cracked in his fourth of the season from close range.

The referee added on 7 minutes of injury time, allowing Hislop to pull off a marvellous save from substitute Birch; Foxe then became injured in a clash of heads and Corica sent a free-kick narrowly wide of the post. Referee Hegley then became centre of attention again, threatening to spoil the game as he sent Pompey manager Harry Redknapp out of his dugout as the drama continued. He then conveniently blew his whistle near the tunnel and ran down the steps to safety, in order to avoid the need for any stewards to escort him from the field.

Portsmouth: Hislop, Crowe, Ritchie, Foxe, Harper, Diabate, Quashie, Taylor, Merson, Todorov, Pericard. Subs: O'Neil, Burchill, Buxton, Robinson, Kawaguchi.
Walsall: Walker, Pollet, Hay, Roper, Bazeley, Sonner, O'Connor, Corica, Wrack, Junior, Leitao. Subs: Birch, Aranalde, Carbon, Simpson, Ward.

HISLOP THE HERO

Date: Saturday 7 December 2002   **Referee:** Tony Leake (Blackburn)
Attendance: 23,462   **Man of the Match:** Shaka Hislop

For three weeks in succession, Pompey had scored three goals to maintain the proud tag of being the leading scorers in all four divisions. Expectation among the 4,511 Pompey supporters who made the short journey to Royal Berkshire was high that they would continue that success, but as they left the ground, it was Pompey's goalkeeper and defence who produced the finer performances and talking points.

A new ground had enticed many Pompey fans – curious to see how a small club like Reading had achieved a magnificent new stadium alongside the M4 motorway. Reading, newcomers from Division Two, were surprising the purists with 6 successive wins behind them, 5 of them by a 1-0 scoreline. This was a meeting between the division's two form sides. The only blot to spoil the day was the Thames Valley Police insisting that the game kicked off at 12 noon.

But preparations for the match had been far from ideal. It had been a tough week for the squad and there was a selection headache for the management team. With winter setting in, colds and 'flu were rife, and several of the Pompey squad, including Shaka Hislop, were dosed up and feeling unwell. Only twelve players had trained the day before, and with injuries and suspensions, Harry Redknapp was reduced to a small squad of players to choose from. De Zeeuw, though, returned from a one-match ban.

The game, which had been over-hyped by the press and media all week, failed to live up to its high profile. In the first half-hour, it appeared both sides were still asleep, the early kick-off on a cold and wet Saturday proving that players are only human. Pompey struggled to break through the Royals' five-man midfield, and by the end of the game they had produced only two shots on target, compared with Reading's three. Shaka Hislop's two diving saves from Forster and Salako, together with Pompey's large army of fans in full voice, complete with the gigantic flag, were the only highlights of the first 45.

A lack of width prompted Harry to bring in Harper for Burchill in the second half, which made an immediate impact. The little Scot's darting runs cutting in from the right started to cause Reading problems, but up front Todorov and Taylor were having an off-day. Despite Reading fielding all three substitutes, the game was not strong on quality from either side, and seldom had Pompey looked so blunt all season. It was the 85th minute when Pompey forced their first of only two corners in the whole match.

With a minute left, the game was summed up when Royals' leading goalscorer Nicky Forster found himself alone 20 yards out with only Hislop to beat, but he kicked the ball straight into the arms of relieved Pompey fans behind the goal. As the largest-ever Madejski Stadium crowd flocked out of the ground to struggle against stationary traffic caused by a fire in the town, it was Pompey who were happier with the point – their first 0-0 of the season and an eighth clean sheet of the

Reading 0   Portsmouth 0

On-loan Scottish defender
Paul Ritchie brightened up
a 0-0 draw in Berkshire.

campaign for Shaka and his defence. Referee Mr Leake delivered a performance as different from the previous Saturday's official as was possible.

Certainly, Hislop and Primus, playing against their old club, had the greatest satisfaction of the match, but questions were raised concerning Pompey's lack of firepower up front, with Todorov and Burchill failing to partner each other well. Deon Burton and Paolo Di Canio were among the players discussed that might be brought in to help boost the squad, with Vincent Pericard out for four to five weeks with a calf injury.

Reading: Hahnemann, Murty, Williams, Upson, Shorey, Rougier, Newman, Hughes, J. Harper, Salako, Forster. Subs: Watson, Cureton, Butler, Tyson, Ashdown.
Portsmouth: Hislop, Primus, Ritchie, Foxe, De Zeeuw, Robinson, Quashie, Taylor, Merson, Todorov, Burchill. Subs: Harper, O'Neil, Crowe, Pitt, Kawaguchi.

Date: Saturday 14 December 2002
Attendance: 13,330

Referee: Peter Walton (Northampton)
Man of the Match: Arjan De Zeeuw/Lassina Diabate

Most seasons, the computerised fixture list produces a match where the return game is just weeks later and, for Pompey, this brought a four-week return to play Stoke City, who had by now lost 9 out of their previous 10 matches. Tony Pulis was having a torrid time. Most of the Pompey talk was of the FA Cup draw away at Old Trafford in January, but 1,711 of Pompey's most loyal supporters were more concerned with the halfway stage of away journeys north to the freezing and depressing wastes of north Staffordshire.

Stoke City moved out of their character-filled Victoria Ground in 1997 to a bleak, concrete industrial estate out of town and a cold, high-positioned Colditz named the Britannia Stadium. For an attendance of just over 13,000, I counted 130 police officers with dogs and riot gear. Outside the ground, on the final whistle, away fans are placed in a caged holding area, no matter what their age, until the all-clear is given to be let out like hungry wolves.

Coupled with the arctic conditions and a biting wind, the freezing fog swirling around the half-empty stadium built on an old slag-heap meant that Stoke was not the place to be for fans and players alike. Deon Burton came straight into the Pompey starting line-up at the expense of Burchill, after his midweek transfer from Derby, to play against the side he had helped to win promotion in a play-off final the previous May. Diabate stood in for Matt Taylor who was suspended. Light freezing drizzle turned to sleet during the first half, which caused Pompey problems, and stud changes soon became necessary. To complete an odd afternoon, around 100 Stoke fans dressed as Elvis made a grand entrance 15 minutes into the match and made for an entertaining distraction.

Pompey missed the penetration of Taylor down the flanks, and it was Stoke who played the better football and adapted better to the horrid conditions. Paul Merson had a quiet match, suffering from the pain-killing injections he was taking as a result of the injury at Hillsborough. It was no surprise when Stoke took the lead on 32 minutes as Pompey looked half-asleep, just as they had done at Reading the previous week. From a free-kick 30 yards out, full-back Thomas was unmarked and had time to push a ball in to Shtaniuk at the far post, who nodded the ball back for Gunnarsson to head in past Hislop. Pompey were all at sea and needed to regroup before Stoke scored again.

Harry Redknapp saw what was needed and made a double substitution at half-time, changing to a wing-back formation. Ritchie and Robinson were replaced by Crowe and Harper, and Linvoy Primus slotted into the back three again. With Harry on the touchline, Pompey started to show signs of turning the game around, and it was Stoke who looked the more tense as the sleet fell more steadily. Pompey possession increased and, on 72 minutes, an equaliser came through intelligent play from Primus. Harper broke down the left and laid the ball in for Linvoy, who

Stoke City 1	Portsmouth 1
Gunnarsson	*Crowe*

'Toddy' appeals to the referee at freezing Stoke.

cleverly slipped the ball over a defender and stabbed a shot past Stoke 'keeper Banks. The ball was about to cross the line, but it was substitute Crowe who made sure that it did for his fourth of the season.

Harper was inspired by the equaliser and was unlucky shortly afterwards when Banks denied him a goal, forcing the ball behind. Suddenly, Pompey looked capable of collecting all 3 points, with Burton, Quashie and Burton again all firing in shots, but although Stoke had not won a game since September, a draw was a fair result to maintain Pompey's healthy lead at the top. This match was the halfway mark of the season, and having collected 53 points (their final tally from the previous season), driving back hurriedly down the M6 to warmer climes, there was plenty to dwell on.

Stoke City: Banks, Thomas, Handyside, Shtaniuk, Hall, Gudjonsson, Gunnarsson, Neal, Henry, Cooke, Greenacre. Subs: Marteinsson, Goodfellow, Mooney, Iwelumo, Cutler.
Portsmouth: Hislop, Primus, Ritchie, Foxe, De Zeeuw, Robinson, Quashie, Diabate, Merson, Todorov, Burton. Subs: Harper, Crowe, O'Neil, Burchill, Kawaguchi.

SHAKA PULLS THE TRACTOR

Date: Saturday 21 December 2002
Attendance: 19,130

Referee: Graham Barber (Hertfordshire)
Man of the Match: Shaka Hislop

On a football Saturday renowned for Christmas shopping, Pompey's highest attendance of the season packed into the old ground, shrouded in mist, to take on ex-Premiership side Ipswich; a club not beaten at Fratton Park since October 1966. Pompey chairman Milan Mandaric made a pitch announcement before the game started, revealing plans of a revamped Fratton Park Stadium, costing £35 million, which is to have 35,000 seats by 2007.

Steve Stone and Matt Taylor returned to Pompey's side to help revert to the wing-back system, and the winter use of an orange ball was paramount as fog descended all over the ground. The almost full-house atmosphere chants of 'Blue Army' and the Pompey Chimes set the game up to be a pre-festive cracker and, happily, it was. Merson set up some good moves, which Quashie and then Todorov pursued, but Diabate brought matters down to earth by collecting his seventh booking of the season for a clumsy tackle on Clapham.

Marshall in the Ipswich goal pulled off a flying save from a 25-yard smash from Todorov, and it was the persistence of the Bulgarian who put Pompey into a 1-0 lead on 19 minutes. The ball took a ricochet out to Taylor in the Ipswich box, who fired in a first-time shot that Marshall could only parry into the path of Todorov, who struck home his twelfth goal of the season from close range. The fog began to swirl, reducing visibility, which brought back memories to older Pompey fans of some pea-souper matches in the 1940s and '50s.

The Tractor Boys began to find their rhythm and missed two good chances, placed over the Fratton End bar. It was now Paul Merson's turn for an off-day, as he gave the ball away three times to the visitors, but Hislop cleared up any danger. Richard Naylor fired a shot against the bar after a goal-mouth scramble just before half-time. Pompey were unlucky not to increase their lead shortly after the interval, when Taylor's right-footed cross curled into the box past everyone, beat Marshall but came back off the post and landed behind Stone.

Ipswich counter-attacked to balance an entertaining match and, on 54 minutes, Magilton won a corner from which he curled in a cross for Gaardsoe to head down a powerful ball low into the corner of Hislop's net. The game then featured action at both ends, with several chances being scorned, Taylor placing a right-foot shot narrowly wide and Todorov shooting just past the far post. Ipswich should have taken the lead when Counago completed a hat-trick of misses as he fired over the bar from 6 yards.

Shaka Hislop then boosted an extraordinary match of chances with magnificent saves at the feet of Marcus Bent at the far post, before diving to claw a Matt Holland header away to safety. Both Pompey and Ipswich threw on fresh legs in the shape of Burchill and Darren Bent, and in the final 15 minutes, the crowd had even more to talk about. Pompey had a goal disallowed for offside, Ipswich defender Chris

Portsmouth 1	Ipswich Town 1
Todorov	*Gaardsoe*

Steve Stone, in typical pose, holds off an Ipswich midfielder at misty Fratton Park.

Makin was sent off for fouling Burchill, Marshall pulled off a great save to keep out Burchill's brave header, Ipswich wing-back Wilnis was stretchered off wearing a neck brace, and one of the referee's assistants pulled a muscle to be replaced by the fourth official!

Although Leicester had closed the gap to 3 points, Pompey were still 12 points clear of third spot, which, as Harry pointed out afterwards, was more important. Ipswich were by far the best side to visit Fratton Park so far in the season, and a draw was no disgrace. The only disappointment of the afternoon was Merson responding to being substituted in the 74th minute by choosing to throw his captain's armband down in a fit of rage and storm up to the dugout in a temper. Frustration and pain had really set in.

Portsmouth: Hislop, Primus, Foxe, De Zeeuw, Stone, Diabate, Quashie, Taylor, Merson, Todorov, Burton. Subs: O'Neil, Burchill, Harper, Ritchie, Kawaguchi.
Ipswich Town: Marshall, Holland, Gaardsoe, Makin, Wilnis, Miller, Magilton, Clapham, Hreidarsson, Naylor, Counago. Subs: M.Bent, D. Bent, Pullen, Wright, Ambrose.

FOUR-DRAW WOBBLE

Date: Thursday 26 December 2002
Attendance: 19,217

Referee: Lee Cable (Woking)
Man of the Match: Matthew Taylor/Shaka Hislop

The traditional, and very eccentric, English gaggle of games over Christmas and New Year started for Pompey on Boxing Day with the first of three matches in under a week. Why do we do it? While other countries take it easy during the holiday week of religious festivity, the Football League pile on the games and the football public love it. Do the players? Answer: yes.

With Crowe in for Stone (hamstring), the Pompey team ran out onto a pitch soggy from the previous day's rain to be greeted by another large holiday crowd, who had travelled despite there being no public transport. Again, expectation was high; the majority of Pompey's support had broken away from Christmas wrapping paper and in-laws to see if a mid-table Palace team could be beaten and hopefully watch their rarely-top-at-Christmas side swing back into winning ways. The pressure was immense. In relegation, the will to win is high, but when a club like Pompey sets out their stall early by going top in August and breaking some records, when they then fail to win a few games, some of those who help pay the wages can be horribly cruel. Pre-match talk in the pubs was of 'a win to get back on track' or 'a defeat to start the collapse of the season'.

Injuries, suspensions and a small squad aside, Pompey cranked into first-half gear brightly, with Todorov slamming an angled shot against the bar from a partially-cleared corner, while Paul Merson saw a lob take a deflection and float just over the woodwork. In the 27th minute, a charge down the wing from Matt Taylor at blistering pace, which totally bypassed Palace midfielder Tommy Black, produced a perfect low cross for Paul Merson to roll in at the far post for his seventh goal of the season. 1-0. Not bad for a guy not fully fit, the wrong side of thirty and on pain-killers for his sore ankle.

The lead only lasted 4 minutes. The Crystal Palace team had height in numbers, which had already caused a few problems. With former Pompey defenders Kit Symons and Shaun Derry in their side, against the run of play, Julian Gray arrived unmarked at the far post and drilled Danny Butterfield's cross first time around Shaka. Pompey then became nervy, the Fratton End sang songs to wind up the totally silent Palace supporters, and half-time arrived.

When Vincent Pericard replaced Deon Burton after 57 minutes, it drew loud applause from the Pompey fans, who were pleased to see the Frenchman back after a month sidelined with a calf injury. He added power up front, but it was the further substitution of O'Neil for a fading Diabate that woke up Pompey's midfield. From 20 yards out, the England Under-20 captain evaded the Palace 'keeper's fingertips and thumped the bar with a fierce shot, which so deserved a goal.

However, for the fourth match in succession, it was Pompey's custodian who pulled off the save of the day. Shaka Hislop had been the difference between defeats and draws in the last three games; this time, he sprawled his large, tall frame

Portsmouth 1	Crystal Palace 1
Merson	*Gray*

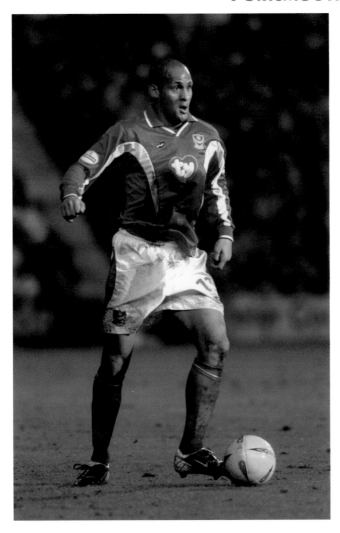

Nigel Quashie pictured in highly concentrated mood on Boxing Day.

low to his right to deny Ade Akinbiyi a goal, which drew applause from the Nigerian himself. Hayden Foxe and Matt Taylor later had chances foiled, both of them having an outstanding match, but many in the 19,000-strong crowd still went home muttering at the final whistle. These people are difficult to please. If 4 successive draws was Pompey's wobble, I'd settle for that. Still picking up points, avoiding defeat is not a bad course for a team that, agreed, were not playing as well as they had been. Pompey's spark was temporarily missing, but with both Leicester and Norwich losing at home, Pompey were still 4 points clear of second spot and 10 points from third.

Portsmouth: Hislop, Primus, Foxe, De Zeeuw, Crowe, Diabate, Quashie, Taylor, Merson, Todorov, Burton. Subs: Pericard, O'Neil, Harper, Burchill, Kawaguchi.

Crystal Palace: Kolinko, Symons, Powell, Popovic, Butterfield, Mullins, Derry, Riihilati, Gray, Adebola, Black. Subs: Akinbiyi, Williams, Routledge, Borrowdale, Micholopoulos.

Date: Saturday 28 December 2002   **Referee:** Chris Foy (Merseyside)
Attendance: 28,165   **Man of the Match:** Arjan De Zeeuw

The first of three away games in a week and Sky TV's presence drew only 1,210 Pompey fans to the fine city of Nottingham, but what a performance they were treated to. Despite Paul Merson missing from the line-up for the first time in the season to rest his injured ankle, Pompey proved to the cynics they were able to play well – and win – without their creative captain. Quashie wore the armband, and O'Neil took his place. Kevin Harper started down the right flank instead of Jason Crowe, who was dropped, and Steve Stone was ruled out of playing against his old side with a hamstring injury.

Pompey kicked off at 5.35 p.m. – the first of five successive abnormal kick-off times – and it was Deon Burton who opened well using his fast pace to pass to Taylor, but his low cross skidded across the face of the goal. Forest's early running was disrupted when they lost Des Walker, and it was the lucky gold shirts of Pompey who began to command the game. After near chances from Burton and Quashie, Pompey claimed a perfect goal when Arjan De Zeeuw powered in a header from close range, but the 1-0 lead was ruled out for pushing by referee Foy, which seemed very harsh.

The first half had been filled with both promise and frustration, and it was disappointing for Pompey not to be in the lead, but their efforts were rewarded with a spectacular goal on 56 minutes, which had the whole ground buzzing. O'Neil broke forward and fed a lovely cross-ball to Matthew Taylor, who cut back on his right foot and curled an incredible 25-yard shot into the corner of the Forest net. Pompey fans went wild behind the goal as Taylor milked the tumultuous applause from the fans having put his side into a deserved lead.

Nottingham Forest, despite having 21-goal David Johnson up front, were woeful and were booed by their own supporters, as Quashie, O'Neil and Harper all went close with chances that either went close or were cleared off the line. With 10 minutes left, Pericard came on for Harper and, with just 3 minutes to go, the Frenchman increased Pompey's lead. Crowe, who had swapped for Burton, broke away down the right and struck a firm shot to show his continued goalscoring ability; Forest 'keeper Ward got a hand to it, but allowed Pericard to run in and push the ball over the line.

In the last minute, Forest won a corner from which defender Dawson dived headlong into the net to score, but the final whistle blew shortly afterwards to bring applause from Pompey's fans, and the anoraked-Paul Merson ran onto the pitch to congratulate the team on a grafted for and confident win. It was Pompey's eighth away win before the turn of the year and their seventeenth win in just 26 League games. The win also showed Pompey were 16 points ahead of the sixth play-off spot, sending a firm message to the rest of the League that 'Pompey mean business this season'.

Nottingham Forest 1
Dawson

Portsmouth 2
Taylor
Pericard

All together now. Toddy, Pericard, O'Neil, Foxe and Diabate celebrate the Frenchman's goal.

Man of the Match Arjan De Zeeuw particularly shone in a solid back three of Foxe and Primus. Todorov and Taylor's skill showed continued growth and the unusual statistic of Pompey having beaten Nottingham Forest in the last 4 meetings in succession, home and away for two seasons running, gave Pompey fans an even more satisfying journey home.

Nottingham Forest: Ward, Louis-Jean, Dawson, Walker, Brennan, Prutton, G. Williams, Reid, Lester, Jess, Johnson. Subs: Doig, Thompson, Westcarr, Roche, Bopp.

Portsmouth: Hislop, Primus, Foxe, De Zeeuw, Harper, Diabate, Quashie, Taylor, O'Neil, Todorov, Burton. Subs: Pericard, Crowe, Robinson, Burchill, Kawaguchi.

Matt Taylor fires a contender for goal of the season at Nottingham.

'This is brilliant', says assistant manager Jim Smith to first-team coach Kevin Bond at the City Ground.

Date: Wednesday 1 January 2003
Attendance: 15,048

Referee: Paul Rejer (Worcestershire)
Man of the Match: Kevin Harper

Pompey ended 2002 at Forest far more happily than they did 2001, when they endured a miserable defeat at Cleethorpes. Away matches were a problem back then, when Pompey travelling anywhere seemed to spell doom, but the trip to Hertfordshire for a New Year's Day televised meeting with Watford was eagerly-awaited despite rain at Vicarage Road for the second year running. The pitch resembled a gluey, sticky toffee pudding as it had been used by Saracens Rugby Club just days earlier.

Unchanged from their 2-1 win at Nottingham, another teatime kick-off saw Pompey fans' stomachs rumbling as poor Arjan De Zeeuw hobbled off the field after just 5 minutes with torn knee ligaments from a hard block tackle from Heidar Helguson. Crowe quickly settled into his place and Pompey defended stoutly with no signs of being unsettled so early. Recording just 2 defeats all season – losing only once on the road – Pompey controlled the first half well, with Quashie thriving on the captain's responsibility. He narrowly missed scoring a goal from Burton's pass, denied by the Watford 'keeper's legs. Todorov and Harper placed shots just past Chamberlain's post, and Taylor poked a shot wide in an entertaining first 45 minutes that just lacked a goal.

It was, therefore, a surprise when Watford took a second-half lead in the 51st minute. Crowe, rarely caught in possession, was beaten by Jermaine Pennant, leaving Pompey open for Micah Hyde to simply tap in from a yard out. But, as so often this season, Pompey – playing in their third strip of all white – responded quickly. On 54 minutes, Kevin Harper, playing in a comfortable wing-back role, fed a through-ball to Todorov in the box, who linked with Quashie to cross for Burton to score from close range and net his first goal since returning to Pompey. 1-1.

Just 4 minutes later, the match had sprung into life, bringing the goal-action the first half had lacked. Kevin Harper chose to somehow execute a virtual carbon copy of the goal he had scored at the Milton End against Norwich a year previously. He raced towards the box and unleashed a magnificent curling shot low beyond the Watford 'keeper into the corner of the net – 2-1, and the 2,283 Pompey fans behind the net Kevin Harper had just scored in went wild.

Pericard came on as a substitute for Burton in the 60th minute to add strength to Pompey's quick-fire response. On top of a muddy morass, Pompey played neat passing football and were heading for all 3 points. But Watford's strength appeared to be producing high crosses, which they fed in all evening, placing Pompey under a constant barrage of pressure. In the last 15 minutes, Neil Cox glanced home a header from Helguson's flick-on to equalise and send the Hornets fans into raptures. Watford were a far better side than the one seen at Fratton six months previously.

Was it a point gained or 2 points dropped? Pompey had a penalty appeal turned down in injury time and Shaka Hislop saved low from Vernazza. On the balance of

Watford 2	Portsmouth 2
Hyde	*Burton*
Cox	*Harper*

'Play on'. referee Paul Rejer allows Gary O'Neil to start another raid at Vicarage Road.

play, it was a fair result as Watford had tried very hard in the last quarter. Festa, Howe, Hughes and now De Zeeuw were all out injured, it was a result achieved by digging deep – overall, it was satisfactory to see Pompey unbeaten in 11 games and kick off the new year with continued creative style and hard work in anticipation of their glamorous cup tie at Old Trafford just three days away.

Watford: Chamberlain, Ardley, Robinson, Vernazza, Cox, Hyde, W. Brown, Noel-Williams, Helguson, Gayle, Pennant. Subs: McNamee, Nielsen, T. Smith, Mahon, Lee.
Portsmouth: Hislop, Primus, Foxe, De Zeeuw, Harper, O'Neil, Diabate, Quashie, Taylor, Burton, Todorov. Subs: Crowe, Pericard, Merson, Stone, Kawaguchi.

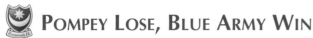

POMPEY LOSE, BLUE ARMY WIN

Date: Saturday 4 January 2003
Attendance: 67,222

Referee: Mike Riley (Leeds)
Man of the Match: Vincent Pericard

FA CUP THIRD ROUND

Pompey were second to last out of the FA Cup draw in December, but the wait was worth it to draw the best English club in Europe and a team that any Nationwide League chairman would rub their hands together just to play against their reserve team. An increase of the usual 2,500-ticket allocation placated 9,000 Pompey fans – only Sky TV spoiled the preparations slightly by choosing a 12.30 lunchtime kick-off which showed little regard for the length of journey Pompey's army had to make to get there.

Yawns aside, it was Pompey's support who won the day and the headlines. Famous for our noise, chanting and singing, which has generally ceased in many of the Premiership grounds now, this was our chance to show the football nation Pompey's twelfth man – our strength of vocal support. The Blue Army, situated in two sections of the ground, were in party mood before kick-off and as the ticker tape fell like snow, the Pompey supporters' noise and songs throughout the game drew praise and comment from the media in the magnificent Old Trafford stadium.

The match took a predictable route, with United showing their superior strength through so many quality players, but, overall, the scoreline flattered them. The game at one stage looked as though it could have reached 6-0, but Pompey dug deep and for half an hour played as well as the supporters cheered. Loan signing from Arsenal, Stathis Tavlaridis, made his debut in place of De Zeeuw, with Steve Stone and Paul Merson returning to the side from injury, relegating O'Neil and Burton to the bench. The start could not have been worse. Linvoy Primus brought down Ryan Giggs for a penalty after 4 minutes – Van Nistelrooy doesn't miss those; 1-0 to United. On 17 minutes, with Pompey fans out-shouting United followers, Diabate brought down Gary Neville 25 yards out and Beckham, inevitably, struck the free-kick which swirled perfectly into Hislop's net, 2-0.

The next 20 minutes bore all the hallmarks of an avalanche, as United fired no less than ten attempts on goal with Pompey not managing to get a sniff. But with 6 minutes left of a one-sided first half, Quashie won a free-kick 40 yards out, Taylor whipped in the free-kick towards the far post, which Hayden Foxe rose to meet well in the box, and the ball fell loosely to Stone, who smashed it high into the roof of the net. Cue delirium from the Pompey fans! Half-time soon passed and two fresh pairs of legs emerged; Pericard for Merson and O'Neil for Diabate. Pompey went about the second half in determined fashion; Taylor, Stone and Pericard all had good shots saved by United 'keeper Carroll. An equaliser nearly came on 62 minutes when Taylor crossed for Pericard, who laid the ball back for Todorov, but he swivelled and scooped his shot over the bar.

Manchester United 4	Portsmouth 1
Van Nistelrooy (2 penalties)	*Stone*
Beckham, Scholes	

It's mine! Pompey's Kevin Harper keeps United's Ryan Giggs at bay.

Gary O'Neil even caught United's defence square, allowing Quashie to run through with only Carroll to beat. Nine times out of ten, he would have scored, but nerves caught up and he lifted his shot over the bar. Further chances for Taylor, Todorov and Pericard went wide, and it took another Van Nistelrooy penalty in the 81st minute to end the game as a contest, Foxe as perpetrator making contact with van Nistlerooy's leg as well as the ball. In the final minute, Tavlaridis was caught out by a long ball over the top, which Scholes raced on to, before floating the ball over Hislop to make the final score on paper somewhat deceptive.

Pompey had given the Premiership giants a tussle, and the sight of England skipper David Beckham walking over to salute and clap Pompey's massive support was an indication of recognition towards some of the finest supporters in the country. The attendance of 67,222 was also the highest crowd any Pompey team had played in front of in a first-team match since the 1939 FA Cup Final, making it the highest crowd listed outside a final in Pompey's entire history.

Manchester United: Carroll, Ferdinand, Blanc, G. Neville, Silvestre, Keane, P. Neville, Richardson, Beckham, Van Nistelrooy, Giggs. Subs: Stewart, Scholes, W. Brown, Forlan, Ricardo.

Portsmouth: Hislop, Primus, Foxe, Tavlaridis, Diabate, Harper, Taylor, Stone, Quashie, Merson, Todorov. Subs: Pericard, O'Neil, Burton, Crowe, Kawaguchi.

POMPEY LOSE, BLUE ARMY WIN

Down you go. Lassina Diabate fells Gary Neville at Old Trafford.

Linvoy Primus outjumps Ryan Giggs in Pompey's memorable cup tie in January.

BLADES STEAL THE SHOW

Date: Monday 13 January 2003
Attendance: 18,872

Referee: Clive Wilkes (Gloucester)
Man of the Match: Linvoy Primus

Although out of the FA Cup at the first hurdle again, Pompey supporters were pleased to hear of two possible signings emerging to strengthen a relatively small and injured squad. The Tim Sherwood deal with Spurs was nearing completion, and twenty-one-year-old Nigerian striker Yakubu Aiyegbeni was to be an exciting loan signing. Meanwhile, a frozen pitch resulted in no weekend football for Pompey, but the game was hastily rearranged for Monday night at Fratton Park, which gave armchair viewers their fourth successive dose of square-eye Pompey.

Gianluca Festa was back in favour of Tavlaridis, and another large floodlit crowd looked forward to an interesting tussle with high-riding Sheffield United, who were in third place in the League but 13 points behind Pompey. A minute's silence was spared for Pompey's record goalscorer Peter Harris, who had recently died at the age of seventy-eight. The Blades lived up to their reputation of being a tough side to beat, and the first half proved to be just so, as Pompey missed several chances before United took the lead on 24 minutes. A high-octane match had the crowd on the edge of their seats, seeing Taylor, Merson and Todorov all go close. But United's talented Michael Tonge sprinted away to play a neat one-two with Michael Brown, before releasing for Peter Ndlovu to control unmarked and accurately slip the ball past Hislop.

Both sides continued to entertain, with Brown's 38th-minute one-on-one strike being pushed on to the upright by Hislop providing another scare for Pompey. Three times in the first half, Matthew Taylor met far-post headers which drifted wide, O'Neil's header hit the bar and, after the interval, Pericard was most unlucky with a fierce shot that appeared to be goalbound, but it hit the far post and rolled away. It was then Paul Merson's turn to join the list of near misses when his 25-yard free-kick cracked the bar in the 76th minute.

A mere 2 minutes later, though, Pompey were deservedly level. Todorov skilfully opened up the United defence for Gary O'Neil to run through and put away a classy goal to equalise. Under manager Neil Warnock, Sheffield were a typically aggressive and physical side, and when Michael Brown earned a yellow card for a wicked late challenge, which should have been red, the Fratton End booed incessantly as Festa was eventually stretchered off with a knee injury.

With so many chances missed, insult was added to injury when referee Wilkes turned down what looked a cast-iron penalty on 83 minutes, as Blades defender Page deliberately handled a header from Pericard that was flying across the goalmouth. Televised highlights proved afterwards the referee missed the contact. Worse followed, with just 3 minutes left. Tavlaridis (who had replaced Festa) missed a long ball in a challenge with Allison, and Ndlovu's dominance knocked Foxe back to miss clearing a header. The ball fell for the much-booed Michael Brown to slam home and celebrate in front of the Fratton End to add double irritation to

Portsmouth 1	Sheffield United 2
O'Neil	*Ndlovu*
	M. Brown

Gary O'Neil surpasses Blades midfielder Michael Tonge.

Pompey's fans in conceding a late goal that became the winner when the game should have been sewn up and won with so many chances missed.

Pompey supporters left the ground in shock. United were now 14 games unbeaten and only 10 points behind. Even United manager Neil Warnock told the press after the game that he thought a draw would have been a fair result. Harry was furious both about the penalty being turned down and about Pompey's lack of concentration in the dying minutes.

Portsmouth: Hislop, Primus, Foxe, Festa, O'Neil, Merson, Quashie, Taylor, Stone, Todorov, Pericard. Subs: Harper, Tavlaridis, Burton, Diabate, Kawaguchi.

Sheffield United: Kenny, Jagielka, W. Quinn, Allison, Montgomery, M. Brown, Murphy, McCall, Page, Ndlovu, Tonge. Subs: Kozluk, Ten Heuvel, Kabba, Peschisolido, G. Smith.

Date: Saturday 18 January 2003   **Referee:** Matt Messias (York)
Attendance: 6,848   **Man of the Match:** Nigel Quashie

From the great to the very small. Pompey's largest away support since 1992 had hauled themselves up to Old Trafford the previous week but, due to Brighton's temporary home, just 756 of them made the forty-mile journey along the A27 to Withdean. This was a strange day all round for a number of reasons. There was no normality to the day whatsoever in this Sussex *v.* Hampshire 'derby'. There was still no standard three o'clock kick-off, with Sussex Police instructing that there should be a 12 noon start to postpone everyone's lunch. No one could park within two miles of the ground. The top team were playing against the bottom side, but the gap in class didn't show. The referee came all the way down from North Yorkshire; one of his assistants wore a baseball cap because of the bright sun and the match was played in an athletics stadium. Unorthodox indeed.

Immediate sympathy was felt by Pompey fans, stuck up in a corner themselves in temporary seating, towards Seagulls season-ticket holders. Bereft of the Goldstone Ground, their temporary home – although nearer than borrowed Gillingham – lacked any atmosphere whatsoever. Suffering a tedious park-and-ride scheme each home game, they arrive at an athletics stadium and tennis court set in a valley of trees and forest where Steve Ovett made his name, rather than any footballer. It was a surreal feeling to watch the game where players shouting instructions could be heard during the match, similar to reserve games. No club with such a history as Brighton deserves this.

The match followed this strange pattern. It was poor. Brighton, struggling at the bottom of their new League, raised their game, as many of Pompey's opponents had this season. A total of 40 points separated the two sides, but there was little proof of that in the first half. Apart from a penalty appeal which was turned down, when Todorov fell in the box after his ankle was clipped, and Zamora showing lively play, the bookings of Tavlaridis, Stone and Watson were the main events up until 12.45 p.m.

Kevin Harper replaced Steve Stone, who suffered from a recurrence of his hamstring injury, and he found Quashie soon into the second half, who released a fierce shot that came back off the foot of the post. But it was Brighton who took the lead on 54 minutes. Paul Brooker, by far the Seagulls' best player in this match, hoofed a ball over Pompey's defence, which Bobby Zamora took in his stride, shook off Tavlaridis and Primus and hit the ball past Hislop from just inside the area, 1-0.

Nigerian international Yakubu warmed up to replace Pericard and set about livening up the Pompey team. His first touches, with the use of both feet and alert positioning, were a delight to watch in a dull game. His presence nearly brought a goal on 62 minutes as he found space with three defenders around him to hit a shot from 18 yards, which Brighton 'keeper Roberts could only parry away. But in the

---

Brighton & Hove Albion 1   **Portsmouth 1**
Zamora   *Todorov*

Brighton & Hove Albion *v.* Portsmouth

Seagulls 'keeper Roberts clips Toddy's ankle, but no penalty was given at Withdean.

64th minute, Pompey were level. Matthew Taylor and Nigel Quashie combined on the edge of the area to feed Todorov, whose familiar sharp turn and swivel-shot firmly zipped past Roberts to make it 1-1.

The goal obviously lifted Pompey, as Yakubu reached the byline 3 minutes later and crossed for Diabate, whose header flew narrowly past the post. By the end of the game, which was played on a sticky, muddy pitch, Brighton had achieved only four shots on target to Pompey's three, and the awarding of a point each was about fair. Overall, Pompey had created few openings, but they were cheered later in the afternoon after hearing that Leicester had lost at Gillingham to ensure Pompey's 5-point lead at the top still stood. The result also meant that Pompey's away record showed the proud statistic of having lost only once in 15 away trips.

Brighton & Hove Albion: Roberts, Watson, Mayo, Cullip, Oatway, Brooker, Carpenter, Pethick, N. Jones, Zamora, Barrett. Subs: Blackwell, Kitson, Piercy, Packham, Hart.

Portsmouth: Hislop, Primus, Foxe, Tavlaridis, Stone, Merson, Quashie, Taylor, Diabate, Todorov, Pericard. Subs: Harper, Yakubu, Crowe, Burton, Kawaguchi.

Debut Double Day

Date: Saturday 1 February 2003
Attendance: 19,428

Referee: Tony Bates (Stoke-on-Trent)
Man of the Match: Yakubu Ayegbeni

Increasing demand to see Pompey play matches at home against sides like Grimsby gave Pompey's ticket office the chance to sell more Milton End seats to Pompey supporters, and with 312 Town fans squeezed into the scoreboard corner, the dry but wintry afternoon brought the largest attendance of the season, all packed in to see another top versus bottom clash.

Without a game for a fortnight, due to being knocked out of the cup, the Pompey team came out refreshed from a short break abroad, and Harry gave home debuts to Yakubu Ayegbeni and Tim Sherwood. Tim had only spent two days training with Pompey since his off-on saga of signing until the end of the season had finally been dealt with in midweek. With the eastern half of the country blanketed in snow, Portsmouth was of mild temperature in contrast, and the fans' mood was to demolish a Grimsby side against whom they had gone top in August. If Pompey were serious about promotion, it was sides like Grimsby from whom they should take 6 points.

A dream start after just 4 minutes got the large crowd fired up before they had even settled. A Grimsby corner fell straight to Paul Merson, who fed Todorov with a delightful flick from the outside of his boot. The Bulgarian showed his pace to burst away from Grimsby shirts and passed a through-ball to Yakubu on the edge of the box. The Nigerian, with poise and precision, shook off his nearest defender and fired a shot in low past Grimsby 'keeper Danny Coyne for 1-0. The buzz around the ground was lengthy, as Pompey fans began to realise what a fast and alert player the man who had experienced Champions League football with Maccabi Haifa was.

Coyne was to be instrumental in keeping the score down. The Welsh international was by far Grimsby's best player, as he kept out chances from Todorov, Yakubu again, Merson and Sherwood. Pompey created several chances in the first half to increase their lead, but Harper shaving the post, Sherwood shooting narrowly wide and Todorov being given off-side gave a false sense of dominance, as Pompey were a class apart from their eastern visitors but had only a slim lead to show for it.

In the second half, an air of complacency seemed to bug the Pompey team, with only half-chances being created and too many passes going astray. Sherwood's debut was generally quiet, but he showed signs of his long experience by splaying out some good midfield balls to Harper and Taylor. Whilst Grimsby never looked dangerous, Pompey's lead was slim and the crowd began to get impatient. It was not until the 75th minute that a sigh of relief could be heard. Kevin Harper's cross cleared the penalty area for Matthew Taylor to neatly collect, control and hammer in a low cross towards a packed penalty area, only for the ball to cannon into the net off the Grimsby full-back Simon Ford for an own goal. 2-0.

Portsmouth 3
Yakubu, Ford (own goal)
Quashie

Grimsby Town 0

Eye on the ball. Debut man Tim Sherwood settled into life at Pompey quickly.

With 9 minutes left, Todorov should have made it 3-0 when he had a free header with no one near him, but he placed the ball wide. Hislop made a flying leap of a save to stop a consolation goal from Grimsby's Mansaram, and Yakubu had a header saved as Pompey piled forward to increase their on-target chances to double figures. However, in stoppage time, Nigel Quashie stamped the authority the scoreline deserved when he raced on to Merson's ball and slammed a shot past Coyne to send everyone home happy, with Pompey's second double of the season. The knowledge of 63 points at the start of February – with only Pompey's first home win since November – was a comforting thought.

Portsmouth: Hislop, Primus, Tavlaridis, Foxe, Harper, Taylor, Sherwood, Quashie, Merson, Yakubu, Todorov. Subs: Crowe, Diabate, Burton, Pericard, Kawaguchi.
Grimsby Town: Coyne, McDermott, Gallimore, Ford, Chettle, Groves, Bolder, Mansaram, Campbell, Santos, Livingstone. Subs: Parker, Cooke, Soames, Ward, Allaway.

Date: Saturday 8 February 2003
Attendance: 19,503

Referee: Clive Penton (East Sussex)
Man of the Match: Yakubu Ayegbeni

The tally of 18 wins out of 30 matches had inspired many Pompey supporters to talk of giving someone a hiding this season. With the arrival of fast-paced Yakubu to partner sharp-footed Todorov, and the presence of lightning winger Taylor as well as the midfield generals of Merson and Sherwood, one of Pompey's opponents was going to get a hammering soon and not necessarily a poor one. If Grimsby's defence was overrun the previous week, Pompey supporters were in for a treat as Derby's back four were cut to ribbons in an astonishing display of sheer force.

Derby, just 4 points below a play-off place and with 5 away wins themselves, faced an unchanged Pompey side, with Tavlaridis continuing in defence to cover for Festa who was still injured. His one-month loan spell from Arsenal had been extended. Another foreign name for Pompey fans to get their tongues round was Finnish international defender Marcus Heikkinen, signed on a three-month contract, who earned a place on the bench after good reserve performances.

A minute's silence was perfectly observed for former 1948/49 Pompey Championship defender Phil Rookes, who had died in the week at the age of eighty-three, and another 19,000-odd crowd were on their feet again as Pompey scored as early as the 3rd minute. Merson sprayed a characteristic pass out to Matt Taylor, who in turn released Yakubu down the left. The Nigerian deftly beat his opponent and crossed low for Merson to pounce and slam the ball against the Derby bar at the Milton End, where the former England man even had time to get up off the ground and follow the loose ball across the line.

That was the signal for more of the one-way traffic shown in the previous week's match. In the 16th minute, Harper, against his old club, charged down the right and swapped passes with Todorov, before crossing low into the box. The ball found Taylor on the far post; he sneaked a pass back to Yakubu, who buried his shot from 8 yards. Just 6 minutes later, Pompey were 3-0 up as Todorov broke out of defence and passed the ball to Taylor, who calmly rolled his shot past 'keeper Grant. While the Fratton End cynically chanted 'Gregory Out' – aimed at Derby and former Pompey manager John Gregory – leading goalscorer Svetoslav Todorov pushed a shot wide of the post, which should have made the score 4-0. Pompey left the field to a standing ovation at half-time.

Derby had nothing to lose as they came out for the second half, and Elliott managed to turn to skim the ball just past the Milton End post. The Derby manager then drew attention to himself by complaining about a throw-in, and was asked to leave the dugout area by referee Penton. As he took his seat in the stand, Quashie lost the ball to Kinkladze, who scurried forward to the edge of the penalty area and forced Hislop to make a save, the ball rebounding straight to Lee Morris who stroked it in from close range in the 58th minute. The Georgian midfielder spelt danger again on 67 minutes, when his intelligent break put McLeod away, only to

Portsmouth 6
Merson, Yakubu (2)
Taylor, Todorov (2)

Derby County 2
Morris
Kinkladze (penalty)

Svetoslav Todorov scores another goal for Pompey as Derby are swept aside at Fratton.

have his shot cleared off the line by Matt Taylor. However, as the ball broke free, Warren Barton appeared to tumble near Todorov, although no Derby player appealed, and up stepped Kinkladze to put away the penalty. 3-2 and the threatened mauling was over.

But was it? In previous seasons, Pompey would have struggled to make any further impact. It was a year ago this weekend that Pompey had drawn 4-4 with Barnsley. Could they throw this one away? No, with this strong-willed team, they stepped up a gear and finished the job they had emphatically started. In the 73rd minute, Yakubu delivered a fine ball through to Todorov, who ran onto goal with only Grant to beat, and his side-foot beat the 'keeper for his fourteenth goal of the season. A mere 7 minutes later, Todorov returned the favour, from Bulgaria to Nigeria, to cement another classy goal for the Pompey fans – so starved of quality football up until this season – to be enthralled by. Merson collected the ball out of defence and fed Toddy, who raced down the left and picked out Yakubu on the other flank. His perfectly-weighted ball fell to the Nigerian's feet, who, without breaking stride, drilled in a hard, low right-foot shot before celebrating at the Fratton End, 5-2.

With 5 minutes left, Yakubu involved himself in the fourth of six goals, as he linked with Todorov down the left to allow the Bulgarian scorer away in the box. His first shot was saved by Grant, but he pounced on the rebound to score at an acute angle to make it six. Fratton Park chanted for seven, but the final whistle sounded to send the majority home celebrating Pompey's biggest win since Millwall were beaten 6-1 in March 1992. Another double, 66 points, classy goals – this was a match to be proud of.

Portsmouth: Hislop, Primus, Foxe, Tavlaridis, Harper, Sherwood, Quashie, Taylor, Merson, Todorov, Yakubu. Subs: Diabate, Heikkinen, Burton, Pericard, Kawaguchi.
Derby County: Grant, Barton, Elliott, Evatt, Zavagno, Bolder, Lee, Kinkladze, Boertien, McLeod, Morris. Subs: Oakes, Jackson, Ravenelli, Murray, Tudgay.

'Toddy' and 'the Yak' celebrate Pompey's sixth *v.* Derby.

Opposite above: Yakubu Ayegbeni wheels away in delight after scoring one of the best goals seen at Fratton Park this season.

Opposite below: Todorov side-foots past Derby 'keeper Grant to score his fourteenth goal of the season.

Date: Monday 17 February 2003
Attendance: 31,775

Referee: Mike Pike (Barrow-in-Furness)
Man of the Match: Kevin Harper

First *v.* second. Pompey on 66 points, Leicester on 64. Floodlit match. Live television cameras. The Premiership on the horizon for both clubs. Weeks of hype. Pompey, the talk of the football nation outside the big league, top of Division One, picking up points faster than a Gatso speed camera can flash by playing proper football and entertaining the public. Tonight was a revenge mission, against a former Premiership side who generally ground out results by hoofing the ball. This was the much-awaited return match from the water-polo farce at Fratton back in November. The scene was firmly set – even though it was a Monday night and another weekend of no Pompey football.

A total of 2,214 Pompey fans had made the journey to the East Midlands and coped with the rivalry outside the old Filbert Street stadium – where they rarely saw a win – next to the brand new Walkers Stadium, where they were seated in a corner of the bowl. Confident from their 6-2 demolition of Derby, Pompey wore their all-white strip for their first visit to the new ground, and all evening the 2,000 or so southerners outsang the Leicester supporters.

On a bitterly cold night with a strong wind, it was Leicester who took hold of the game, and Pompey found themselves one down after just 9 minutes. Arjan De Zeeuw, chosen for his experience, attempted to clear a ball, which Scowcroft charged down and released to Trevor Benjamin, who snapped up the loose ball and pounded it past Hislop at the near post. Pompey were not deflated. Their support got louder and there was self-belief amongst the team and fans alike that they could bounce back, as they had already done 9 times this season, and come from behind to draw or win. However, Leicester continued to force Pompey back and outmuscle them in midfield with long balls, and the half-time whistle could not come soon enough when Dickov sent a free header just the past the post, unmarked by the white back four.

The second half was different. Whereas Pompey had stood off and allowed the Foxes to play their hoof-it style of football in the first 45, Pompey came out and dominated the second. No team changes; just a determined side, with Kevin Harper in particular exploiting some space and showing City he meant business. Pompey won a string of corners as their confidence grew. Dickov squandered a great chance at the other end when, clean through, he rolled his shot wide; it was the turning point in the match and the signal for Pompey to step up and equalise.

Matthew Taylor showed Paul Dickov how to finish a goal properly. In the sixty-5th minute, he controlled a looping pass from Paul Merson, cut inside past Sinclair and Scowcroft and curled a perfect right-footed belter beyond Walker and in off the woodwork. It was a carbon copy of his goal at Nottingham Forest. Matthew Taylor raced away to the mass of Pompey fans in the corner and impersonated a darts player at the oche, throwing an imaginary arrow to celebrate a memorable goal. It

Leicester City 1	Portsmouth 1
Benjamin	*Taylor*

Yes, it's in. Paul Merson joins in the celebrations at Leicester.

was, without doubt, a precision goal – scored with his right foot, too, when his left one was normally more reliable!

Oddly, Leicester did not push forward. The remaining 25 minutes ticked away, with the home side content with a point. Excellent refereeing from Barrow official Mike Pike let the game flow, and the skill of Sherwood, Quashie and Ze Deeuw pushed Leicester further and further back, which made the large home support even quieter than before. Pompey's fans sang 'We are top of the League', and they nearly saw Pompey win the game when Kevin Harper beat Alan Rogers, but he had no support to take the ball through. In the final minutes, Harper and Taylor again had shots saved, and Quashie sent a free-kick wide for Pompey to finish the stronger of the two sides. Half an hour after the match had finished, the Pompey Army of support could be heard in the ground, singing 'we're gonna win the League', which seemed a fitting finale. The two clubs way out at the top of the division had chased each other all game and, although Leicester had led and gone top for 56 minutes, Pompey's quality and persistence shone through for them to regain their prime spot.

Leicester City: Walker, Sinclair, Elliott, Taggart, Rogers, Scowcroft, Davidson, Izzet, McKinlay, Dickov, Benjamin. Subs: Summerbee, Wright, Stewart, M. Jones, Flowers.

Portsmouth: Hislop, Primus, Foxe, De Zeeuw, Harper, Sherwood, Quashie, Taylor, Merson, Todorov, Yakubu. Subs: Pericard, Diabate, Festa, O'Neil, Kawaguchi.

POETIC JUSTICE

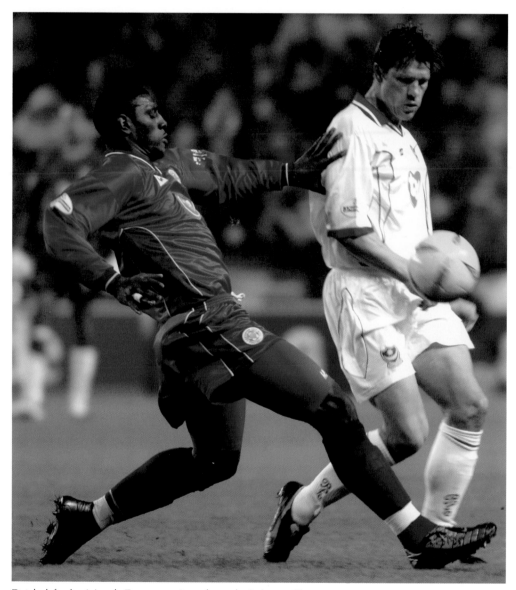

Dutch defender Arjan de Zeeuw remains calm under Leicester City pressure.

Kevin Harper: 'C'mon Matt, 180!'

A DAY OUT FOR MARWELL

Date: Saturday 22 February 2003
Attendance: 19,521

Referee: Steven Dunn (Bristol)
Man of the Match: Arjan De Zeeuw

Following a thumping 6-2 home win, it's never easy to keep the home fans that happy. Expectation was high; street-corner pubs were overflowing on an exceptionally warm and sunny February afternoon as royal blue-shirted drinkers consumed their pints faster than the traffic moved along Milton Road. Talk was of how many Pompey would score today against another mid-table side like Gillingham. The antique turnstiles at Fratton Park creaked as an ever larger attendance of 19,521 poured in.

But football, as we all know, is seldom predictable. The Gills, with 5 away successes on the road, came to defend and the game was not a pretty spectacle. Pompey had one change in the team from the Leicester draw; Festa stepped in, recovered from his injured knee, to replace Hayden Foxe, who was allowed paternity leave to be with his wife for the birth of their first child.

The first half opened as it was to finish, with the red shirts of Gillingham determined to shut out Pompey's effective play. It was to be a game of wits – each time Pompey pressed forward, Todorov or Merson were quickly blotted out. With a swirling wind too, it became a hard, physical game and although both sides forced corners, neither was able to capitalise. Near the stroke of half-time, Kevin Harper broke through the right and crossed for Taylor, who escaped the Gills' close attention for a change, but in cutting back onto his favourite right foot, the England Under-21 international had his low effort saved by 'keeper Brown.

Pompey had more possession in the second half, and with inspired flashes of skill from Quashie, Pompey started to establish a hold over the Gillingham defence. Pompey's enigmatic midfielder hit a fierce 30-yard shot at Brown, which he tipped over the bar. But in the 58th minute, an unlikely scorer to appease the local bookies, put Pompey ahead. From a Paul Merson corner, which he curled to the back post, Arjan De Zeeuw headed the ball back across the goal, past Brown and into the opposite corner of the net.

It was the Dutchman's first goal for Pompey and turned out to be the match-winner; this was unusual as he was not recruited as a goalscorer among the summer bargains snapped up by Harry Redknapp. But they all count and the Fratton End chanted 'Marwell' (a connotation with the Hampshire Zoo) to the likeable and experienced defender, who had recovered from an enforced lay-off caused by a knee ligament injury.

But now it was Pompey's turn for a scare. Former Saint Danny Wallace, who had scored 7 goals in 8 games, threatened on two occasions, but De Zeeuw was back in his normal spot to clear the ball on the first and the supporters' club Player of the Month, Linvoy Primus, tackled cleanly for the second. Hislop was later tested by a long-range shot from Shaw, and De Zeeuw cleared two corners as the visitors upped the pressure.

Portsmouth 1
De Zeeuw

Gillingham 0

Man of the Match Arjan de Zeeuw covered all 110 x 72 yards against Gillingham.

Gillingham's defenders earned applause for closing down Pompey's attack so effectively and Pompey's back four of Hislop, Festa, De Zeeuw and Primus won praise for keeping the Kent side at bay. This was Pompey's tenth clean sheet of the season, and Linvoy Primus and Arjan De Zeeuw were singled out for their exceptional performance; the latter particularly, as he covered every blade of grass on the pitch, mopped up well at the back and scored the winner. Historically, Pompey had also kept up their superb record of never having lost to Gillingham at Fratton Park.

Portsmouth: Hislop, Primus, Festa, De Zeeuw, Harper, Sherwood, Quashie, Taylor, Merson, Todorov, Yakubu. Subs: Pericard, O'Neil, Diabate, Tavlaridis, Kawaguchi.

Gillingham: J. Brown, Nosworthy, Hope, Ashby, Edge, Hessenthaler, P. Smith, Southall, Shaw, Ipoua, Wallace. Subs: Sidibe, Johnson, Perpetuini, Spiller, Bartram.

Date: Saturday 1 March 2003
Attendance: 9,697

Referee: Howard Webb (Rotherham)
Man of the Match: Paul Merson

An undefeated February placed Pompey on 70 points as the team coach – without any fans in tow – motored up the well-worn A3 to skirt south London and play Millwall. A total of 70 points, 40 goals at home, 20 wins in 33 games and just 1 defeat away all seemed surreal to most Pompey fans, the majority of whom were confined to listening to the game on local radio or watching it at Fratton Park on a big screen. The policy of selected visiting fans being banned from the New Den was still in situ, and despite Pompey allowing Millwall fans to Fratton Park in September, the Metropolitan Police stuck to their original plan to reduce any threat of violence in this notorious fixture.

Unchanged from the previous week, Pompey ran out of the tunnel onto a surface made porridge-like by the torrential rain that had fallen a hour before kick-off, which set a miserable scene in this unwelcoming part of south London. A sparse 'home' crowd was dotted about the four empty sides of the concrete ground, whose voices could be heard as though it was a reserve match. The lack of Pompey atmosphere was decidedly eerie, as Pompey started the game brightly against an indifferent Millwall side.

There was no definitive clue beforehand as to what was about to happen, but in just half an hour, a flurry of Pompey goals made the two sides look a class apart. On the quarter-hour, a free-kick from Todorov to Harper was driven in between Merson and Yakubu, who got in a tangle; Millwall defenders stood and watched as the Nigerian slid a low-footed shot past 'keeper Warner. After close misses by Merson and Todorov, 'the Yak' doubled Pompey's lead on 25 minutes. Merson delivered a delightful pass, which opened up the Millwall defence for Toddy to run clear down the left. Yakubu received the square pass to side-foot home with the 'keeper stranded: 2-0. Paul Merson was having a riot as Millwall's midfield could do nothing to prevent his clever play and the space he created. In the 31st minute, Harper exchanged passes with Todorov following another Merson through-ball and this time Tim Sherwood was perfectly placed to score his first Pompey goal at the far post to make it 3-0.

The frustration and petulance of hardman Dennis Wise, now in Lions colours, showed when he ran his studs down Quashie's leg, bringing about a mêlée with Sherwood and Quashie throwing punches in return. Referee Webb yellow-carded Dennis and Nigel. But if the normally intimidating atmosphere of the New Den was in shock at such a one-sided game, they were even more so in stoppage time before the interval. Yet another precision pass from Paul Merson placed Todorov in a perfect position to smash his sixteenth goal of the season from a tight angle for 4-0. Millwall were booed off.

Former Pompey striker and player-manager Steve Claridge had engaged in a quiet first half, but he tried his best in the second against an irresistible Pompey team,

---

Millwall 0

Portsmouth 5
Yakubu (2), Sherwood
Todorov, Merson (penalty)

All smiles as Pompey score their biggest away win for thirty years.

forcing three shots at Shaka Hislop, all to no avail. Millwall had 6 shots on target to Pompey's 4, but all of Pompey's went in! It was that sort of game. With substitutions filling the occasional boredom, it was Pompey who finished the game off in the 72nd minute when they were awarded a clearcut penalty. Taylor had fed Merson down the right who passed to Yakubu in the box. Yakubu was then brought down by Robinson for a penalty. Although the Yak could have wanted his hat-trick, Merson showed no feelings, stepped up and sent Warner the wrong way for his ninth goal of the season. The exit gates opened and Millwall fans flooded out in droves. Pompey should have made it six when Crowe, on for Harper, squared a ball for Todorov in front of an open goal, but the Bulgarian missed the ball. There was still time for Millwall 'keeper Warner to deny Quashie with a leg-save in injury time, as Pompey clocked up their best League away win since February 1973 at Preston.

Millwall had been crushed heavily, not for the first time – Rotherham had scored six at the New Den – and rudely by Pompey, and the smirk had certainly been wiped off the face of the Lions' manager, Mark McGhee. The Millwall fans who were left in the ground, not known for opposition praise, gave Paul Merson a standing ovation as he left the field, which he suitably acknowledged in the hard absence of his own fans. This time a year ago, Pompey had lost 5-0 at The Hawthorns; twelve months later – what a change.

Millwall: Warner, Reid, Ward, Robinson, Ryan, Ifill, Livermore, Wise, Kinet, Claridge, Harris. Subs: Sadlier, Rees, Dunne, Hearn, Gueret.
Portsmouth: Hislop, Primus, Festa, De Zeeuw, Harper, Sherwood, Quashie, Taylor, Merson, Todorov, Yakubu. Subs: Crowe, Pericard, Diabate, O'Neil, Kawaguchi.

Tim Sherwood gets away from Dennis Wise.

Yakubu scored two goals at Millwall and hit the crossbar so hard that it shook for some time.

CUCKOOS PUSH POMPEY OUT

Date: Tuesday 4 March 2003
Attendance: 10,356

Referee: Peter Walton (Northamptonshire)
Man of the Match: Yakubu Ayegbeni

As surreal as football circumstances can be, this one topped the lot. With no fans at Millwall on Saturday, the complete opposite happened at Wimbledon. No fewer than 9,110 of Pompey's exceptional away supporters attended the usually deserted seats of Selhurst Park. Pompey were the highest scorers in any of the four professional divisions, which lured many from the South Coast to the borrowed ground in south Norwood. There was simply no comparison with the scarcity of the home support – it was a gulf of embarrassment.

Dons fans were outnumbered 9-1 by Pompey's massive travelling army; the blue legion alone totalled more than the entire home attendance against Peterborough earlier in the season. But, unfortunately, in true Pompey style – like Liverpool, Villa Park, Sunderland and the City Ground in the '93 play-offs – it turned into an anti-climax and those blue thousands went home disappointed. True, it was only the second away defeat of the season, but a combination of three factors determined the result. A dreadful, over-worn bumpy pitch did not suit Pompey's style of football; complacency set in after a 1-0 lead; and the referee failed to give a blatant penalty.

It all started well, despite a mini injury crisis which saw Kevin Harper sidelined with a calf injury. With no natural right wing-back, Pompey were light in that department but battled on and, on 26 minutes, Nigel Quashie was the instigator when Pompey took the lead. Nigel slipped a through-ball to Todorov, who ran towards goal, but Wimbledon 'keeper Kelvin Davis parried his fierce shot. The ball broke to Quashie, who squared to Paul Merson on the edge of the box for the Pompey captain to smash in and reach double figures in his goal tally for the season.

Pompey suffered more bad luck with injury in the 33rd minute, when defender Jason Crowe limped off with a foot injury to give Harry and Jim the headache of three injured defenders. O'Neil replaced him and Pompey reshuffled, with Festa at right-back and Taylor moved to the left. Mid-table Wimbledon sensed a comeback and having quite often been the surprise team of the week this season with away wins against top sides, they took the game by the scruff of the neck and stepped up a gear.

Volz, Reo-Coker and Ainsworth were outstanding. Pompey lacked width and Ainsworth had Taylor in his pocket. Jobi McAnuff came on for the Dons in the 62nd minute, and within 4 minutes, the Dons had equalised. The signs were there from a succession of corners, with which Shaka Hislop had coped under pressure. But from another corner, a static Pompey defence saw Patrick Agyemang swivel round to meet Shipperley's header to score with his right foot just past Hislop's far-reaching arm. 1-1.

The turning point was 6 minutes from the end when subsequent camera proof showed that Pompey had been denied a blatant penalty. Vincent Pericard, on for

Wimbledon 2	Portsmouth 1
Agyemang	*Merson*
Ainsworth	

Jim Smith, Kevin Bond and Harry Redknapp mutter expletives to each other about Mr Walton.

Todorov, was sent sprawling at the Sainsbury's End under a clumsy challenge from Volz. Pompey appealed, referee Walton chose to speak to his linesman, who was 50 yards away, but Walton turned it down. Cruelly, with just 3 minutes left, Pompey conceded a late goal, having given away possession in midfield. Reo-Coker jigged his way through Pompey's gold shirts and squared for Ainsworth, easily the Don's best player, to score from 12 yards. The few Wimbledon fans left banged empty seats up and down to create some noise in celebration of their late winner. Drizzle fell to accompany the disappointed Pompey Army back home through Mitcham, Merton and Malden.

Wimbledon: Davis, Volz, Andersen, M.Williams, Hawkins, Ainsworth, Morgan, Reo-Coker, Shipperley, Gray. Subs: Agyemang, McAnuff, Darlington, Gier, Gore.
Portsmouth: Hislop, Primus, De Zeeuw, Festa, Crowe, Taylor, Sherwood, Quashie, Merson, Yakubu, Todorov. Subs: O'Neil, Pericard, Diabate, Tavlaridis, Kawaguchi.

Date: Wednesday 12 March 2003   **Referee:** Dermot Gallagher (Banbury)
Attendance: 19,221   **Man of the Match:** Svetoslav Todorov

Matches played under the bright lights in an evening after a working day often seem to bring out extra excitement in the football public. The October home game with Preston had seen four of the five goals scored in the first half – oddly, this match provided five goals all scored in the second half, which had the large crowd up and down in their seats like yo-yos.

The Pompey team were keen to get the defeat of the previous match out their systems and, thanks to Sky TV, had longer to wait than scheduled, as this game was put back by four days. Steve Stone failed a fitness test, Paul Merson played with a heavy cold and Kevin Harper was not fully fit, as Harry and Jim assembled the remnants of an injury-torn squad to take on the yellow-and-green team from Norfolk. Norwich City arrived with 11 defeats behind them, and as they were 7 points short of a play-off place, they had nothing to lose – in fact, pride was at stake as they wanted to try and achieve the double over Pompey.

An anxious first half of mediocre fare for the crowd had few highlights, other than players from both sides hitting shots over the bar. The best chance occurred in the the 36th minute, when Kevin Harper scooped the ball inches wide of goal with the only real opportunity of the half. Both sides struggled to get the game to flow, but a change of formation at the interval changed the whole match. Harper's calf injury flared up again, so Gary O'Neil replaced him in midfield and Pompey switched to a 4-3-1-2 pattern, which made the match explode into life. In the 56th minute, Pompey were in front, as Todorov beat the Norwich offside trap with a perfectly-timed ball for Yakubu to coolly slot away his sixth goal of the season. However, before Pompey fans had sat back down in their seats and Harry had returned to the dugout, City had equalised – within 20 seconds of kick-off! Rivers escaped Taylor down the flank and cross-fed a ball for Clint Easton to nod home. 1-1.

Amazingly, there was hardly any time to retaliate. In the 59th minute, former Norwich City star Tim Sherwood fed Yakubu, who deftly passed through for Todorov to finished clinically, sending the Fratton End into raptures again. However, for a side who had not scored in their last 3 matches, Norwich City turned the game into a nail-biter, as they were level again within 3 minutes. Zema Abbey found too much space in Pompey's half, the normally resilient defence failed to clear and Mark Rivers, the Canaries' best performer, smashed in another equaliser from the penalty-box line to make the score 2-2.

Todorov stole the show 10 minutes later to ensure there was another twist in a pulsating 16-minute spell. In the 72nd minute, Norwich defenders missed Paul Merson's corner and the ball fell into the Bulgarian's path in the 6-yard box. He sent a spectacular volley through a sea of legs which hit the roof of the Fratton End net. Thanks to Shaka Hislop, Pompey managed to hold on as he pulled off a point-blank stop from Abbey's header. There was plenty for the media to talk about, and

Portsmouth 3	Norwich City 2
Yakubu	*Easton*
Todorov (2)	*Rivers*

Toddy celebrates a spectacular volley against Norwich with Matt Taylor.

Pompey left the field to a standing ovation for such a prolific and invigorating display. Their energy, lacking in the first half, had been renewed in the second to provide one of the most exciting periods in any game this season. It was the sort of entertainment fans wanted to see over and over again on video.

But the vital 3 points, which extended their lead at the top to 5, was not without cost. Linvoy had suffered a back injury; De Zeeuw had taken a knock when falling into the South Enclosure concrete; Kevin Harper, Steve Stone and Paul Merson were struggling for fitness; and Nigel Quashie was about to sit out a two-match ban.

Portsmouth: Hislop, Primus, Festa, De Zeeuw, Harper, Sherwood, Quashie, Taylor, Merson, Todorov, Yakubu. Subs: O'Neil, Diabate, Foxe, Pericard, Kawaguchi.
Norwich City: Green, Drury, Mackay, Holt, Abbey, Nedergaard, McVeigh, Russell, Easton, Rivers, Bromby. Subs: Nielsen, Emblen, I. Roberts, Shackell, Crichton.

Pompey supporters' Player of the Season – Mr Solid, Linvoy Primus.

This happy breed. Toddy, the Yak, Foxy and Harps celebrate at Fratton.

GOLDEN OLDIES

Date: Saturday 15 March 2003   **Referee:** Philip Dowd (Stoke-on-Trent)
Attendance: 19,558   **Man of the Match:** Gary O'Neil

The two longest-serving clubs in Division One met on a perfectly crisp, sunny spring afternoon for an old-fashioned type of encounter. Both clubs are steeped in history – most of it with dust on – and both have underachieved in the past decade. However, Portsmouth and Wolves are followed by dyed-in-the-wool supporters, famed for their respective vocal support. Wolves brought a modest 1,594 gold-shirted followers to see the senior experience of Dennis Irwin and Paul Ince square up to Pompey's elder statesmen of Sherwood, Merson, Stone and De Zeeuw.

As a testimony to the quality of football currently being played at Fratton Park, a spare ticket for this match was virtually impossible to find, as a season's best of 19,558 fans crammed into every plastic seat to be found, including fifty new ones beneath the police control box. Lacking key personnel in Nigel Quashie (suspended) and Matt Taylor (ankle injury), Pompey faced a Wolves side who had spent their whole week in the south, having lost a cup tie along the M27 a week previously but having won mid-week at Reading. Harry was aware of Wolves' impressive record away from Molineux as they had won 9 matches – the same as Pompey – and lay comfortably placed in the play-off zone. For this reason, and because of injury problems, Pompey's manager chose to abandon the wing-back formation and play four across the back, with Steve Stone returning from his hamstring trouble and Gary O'Neil starting in midfield for the first time since New Year's Day.

With Wolves unbeaten in the League since January, Pompey expected a stiff test, so it was a surprise to all when they took the lead after just 4 minutes. Showing no signs of easing back in gently after an absence of two months, former England international Steve Stone pounced on a loose ball 40 yards out and charged towards the Milton goal unchallenged, before releasing a fierce shot which Wolves 'keeper Matt Murray could only help on its way into the net. It was a memorable goal and set the pace of the game, encouraging attacking raids from both sides.

But as the clock showed half an hour gone, the frenetic pace wore off and it became a stifled contest with both teams cancelling each other out. The Fratton and North sides of the ground livened up the match with a solid 10-minute rendition of 'Top of the League, Harry and Jim' to the tune of 1980s hit 'Tom Hark' by The Piranhas. Fussy referee Mr Dowd then made the first of five bookings in a match which was never physical, Foxe and Stone receiving yellows.

In the second half, Harper replaced Linvoy Primus and the game became more defensive. Very little got past De Zeeuw, Fox and Festa, while Stone and O'Neil were an inspiration in midfield, supporting Paul Merson (who was below par due to his pain-killing injections) and Tim Sherwood, who snuffed out the threat of Messrs Ince and Irwin, relegating them to near anonymity. Clear openings for either side were scarce, except for Yakubu, who twice raided the Wolves penalty area only to be foiled by Murray.

Portsmouth 1   Wolverhampton Wanderers 0
Stone

'Get off, mate!' Composed central defender Hayden Foxe beat his Wolves opponent, Ludo Pollet.

With three substitutions made in the final 10 minutes, the match reached a satisfactory end with another clean sheet for Shaka and another afternoon's great work for Pompey in securing a total of 6 precious points in three days. Harry Redknapp showed a rare moment of public emotion on the final whistle, punching the air with delight as 79 points in mid-March was a proud number to reach by anyone's standards. As his team left the pitch, a safety evacuation exercise onto the pitch from the North lower stand's occupants provided a snapshot image of one portion of the happy scenes wished for in seven weeks' time.

Portsmouth: Hislop, Primus, Festa, De Zeeuw, Foxe, Sherwod, Stone, O'Neil, Merson, Todorov, Yakubu. Subs: Harper, Burton, Diabate, Pericard, Kawaguchi.
Wolverhampton Wanderers: Murray, Edworthy, Pollet, Clyde, Irwin, Cameron, Rae, Ince, Kennedy, Sturridge, Miller. Subs: Newton, Proudlock, Cooper, Naylor, Oakes.

Date: Wednesday 19 March 2003
Attendance: 13,922

Referee: Michael Ryan (Preston)
Man of the Match: Steve Stone

Not since a Ray Hiron double in February 1965 had Pompey won at Highfield Road. Why, no Pompey team had even scored there since a 2-1 win thirty-eight years previously. But in the thirty-eighth match of the season, Pompey scored three in 9 minutes. Playing in an all-white strip, the pressure was on, as Leicester and Sheffield United had both won the previous night. Although Coventry City had not won a home match since Boxing Day, their more-than-capable midfield looked ominous on paper, and the squad had given Pompey a tough match back at Fratton Park in October.

However, there was no need for concern. The Sky Blues lacked ambition and strength up front and, in short, showed too much respect for Pompey. After Shaka Hislop had saved a volley from Dean Holdsworth in the 13th minute, Pompey took the lead just 60 seconds later. Sky Blues defender Calum Davenport let the ball slip from under his foot for Todorov to steam through on goal. His shot hit the post and rebounded off Gary Caldwell's leg; bad luck for City, but Pompey were on the way to a tenth away win. It was Davenport who was the villain again 3 minutes later, as he lost possession to Yakubu Ayegbeni in the box; sharp-eyed Gary O'Neil and Steve Stone fed each other for the former Forest man to angle in his second goal in four days.

It was not Coventry's night and their agony was prolonged when John Eustace missed the target from 6 yards out, before Pompey scored again in the 23rd minute. Dynamite-driven Yakubu outclassed Coventry defender Craig Pead, and sped like an overtaking motorbike to place a superb cross for the waiting Kevin Harper to roll in his third of the season. 3-0 – three chances, three goals. My watch showed 8.08 p.m. and I thought of exiled Pompey fans around the UK, unable to listen to radio commentary, who might be switching on Teletext for a scoreflash, blinking as they saw 3-0 on their screens!

Coventry tried to come back into the game, but found Pompey's defence too resolute and Shaka in good enough form to save all that was fired at him; Holdsworth, Joachim and Eustace were all his victims. Even though De Zeeuw limped off with an ankle injury, Pompey's wing-back system worked perfectly against McAllister's side; intelligent and incessant runs from O'Neil and Harper had the Coventry midfield perplexed.

Finnish international Markus Heikkinen played comfortably at the back for 65 minutes, replacing De Zeeuw, and Tim Sherwood controlled everything in the engine room. Although City found some resolve in the second half, Pompey always looked the stronger of the two, and it was game over in the 68th minute when captain Paul Merson had a rare moment. Steve Stone, who visibly enjoyed a vigorous performance over the 90 minutes, stormed through into the penalty area and crossed for Toddy, whose knock-back was swept up by Paul Merson who,

---

Coventry City 0

Portsmouth 4
*Caldwell (own goal), Stone
Harper, Merson*

Yakubu Ayegbeni showed the pace of a Yamaha R1 at Coventry.

without pausing, scored with his left foot past the Coventry 'keeper. 4-0, and the former England man had scored with his weaker foot!

Yakubu could have scored a fifth goal late on, after a super pass from Merson, but he shot wide. On the final whistle, Harry Redknapp came out on to the pitch with Jim Smith to salute the 1,922-strong army of Pompey fans who had lapped up every minute of another exciting evening game, another clean sheet and a solid Pompey display. Winning 5-0 and 4-0 away in the same month was heady stuff for Pompey's regular away travellers.

Coventry City: Hyldgaard, Pead, Shaw, Davenport, Caldwell, Eustace, McAllister, Chippo, Safri, Holdsworth, Joachim. Subs: McSheffrey, Whing, Jansen, Engonga, Debec.
Portsmouth: Hislop, Foxe, Festa, De Zeeuw, Harper, O'Neil, Sherwood, Merson, Stone, Todorov, Yakubu. Subs: Heikkinen, Pericard, Diabate, Burton, Kawaguchi.

Date: Saturday 22 March 2003   **Referee:** Matt Messias (York)
Attendance: 16,665   **Man of the Match:** Hayden Foxe

The Pompey squad and management stayed up in the Midlands and the north for two days, rather than return home from Highfield Road only to haul themselves back up to Tom Finney country for Saturday. A gloriously sunny day in Lancashire welcomed the two teams out onto an immaculate Deepdale pitch for what was to be Pompey's last 3 o'clock away kick-off of the season. Linvoy Primus had recovered sufficiently from his pelvic injury to return into the back three to replace Arjan De Zeeuw. Gary O'Neil continued in central midfield, despite Nigel Quashie having finished his 2-match suspension – he was now out because of a dead leg suffered in training.

Preston were yet another mid-table side Pompey faced away from home who seemed determined to raise their game against the League leaders. But by end of the first half, it was Pompey who should have been in a 3-0 lead. Primus found himself in an early scoring position, but volleyed wide after 3 minutes. As soon as Yakubu scored 2 minutes later, for his seventh goal in 10 games, Pompey dominated the half, but scorned too many chances.

The best part of 2,409 loyal Pompey fans had made the long journey north and were still standing up and celebrating when Kevin Harper won possession in the centre circle and traded passes with Steve Stone. Yakubu ran like an express train into the penalty area to meet Stone's pass, and struck the ball low and hard into the opposite corner. Toddy then contrived to shoot wide when swivelling on the loose ball just 3 yards out, while Paul Merson lobbed over from close range with only the Preston 'keeper to beat. It was a profound miss for someone of Merson's calibre, but it happens to every professional.

After the interval, Todorov curled a 20-yard effort narrowly wide, and later sent Gary O'Neil on a mazy run; he shot early, with Preston white shirts all around him, forcing Lucas to save to his right. Defending a 1-0 lead against a home side who had won their last two home games 4-2 and 5-0 was a difficult task, but Hayden Foxe, Gianluca Festa and Linvoy Primus coped well with the lively Preston raids, and Shaka in Pompey's goal mopped up chances from Cresswell, Alexander and Lewis. Whereas the points should have been Pompey's by half-time, the real drama came in the last 2 minutes which meant that the end result felt like a point gained instead of 2 points dropped.

The referee awarded a disputed free-kick on the edge of Pompey's box in the 89th minute. An innocent-looking ball from Alexander rolled across the penalty area, which caught blue-shirted defenders out. Paul McKenna found space and drilled a low 25-yard angled shot through a sea of legs and past Shaka Hislop, prompting jacket-less Harry Redknapp to kick out at a water-bottle near the dugout. 1-1. Sensing Pompey were rattled enough to concede a second, Preston substitute Simon Lynch burst through in injury time in search of a dramatic winner, and hit a

Preston North End 1	Portsmouth 1
McKenna	*Yakubu*

High flier. Tim Sherwood fires at Preston 'keeper David Lucas. Meanwhile, Linvoy's having a laugh.

firm, low shot which Shaka Hislop saved with his left leg. There was even time for another Preston substitute, Mears, to slice a shot wide of the post before the final whistle.

A crop of injuries to Pompey's squad had become as repetitive as painting the Forth Bridge. Taylor, De Zeeuw and Quashie were all sidelined, and Harper and Primus were not 100 per cent fit for this game so, on reflection, it was a good point in a 6-match month for Pompey. Each match of the season was a step towards the ultimate dream, and the thirty-ninth one had been climbed with great endeavour. Hislop, Foxe, Festa and Sherwood were instrumental in Pompey returning south with a proud record of still just 2 away defeats all season.

Preston North End: Lucas, Alexander, Broomes, Lucketti, Edwards, Cartwright, McKenna, Etuhu, Lewis, Cresswell, Koumantarakis. Subs: Lynch, Mears, O'Neil, Lonergan, Skora.
Portsmouth: Hislop, Foxe, Festa, Primus, Harper, O'Neil, Sherwood, Merson, Stone, Todorov, Yakubu. Subs: Burton, Diabate, Clark, Heikkinen, Kawaguchi.

FROM A JACK TO A KING

Date: Saturday 5 April 2003
Attendance: 7,899

Referee: Scott Mathieson (Stockport)
Man of the Match: Kevin Harper

With no match the previous week due to international call-ups, promotion-hungry players and supporters of Pompey were starved by another football-less fortnight. Sky TV prolonged the wait another two hours for a 5.35 p.m. teatime kick-off at Walsall, as Pompey kicked off in their favoured gold away strip, playing their fifth match out of seven on the road. Nigel Quashie returned to first-team action, reducing O'Neil to the bench. Walsall were without four first-choice players through suspension, including on-loan Pompey midfielder Carl Robinson. Placed just above the bottom, their home record had a symmetrical look about it with 9 home wins and 9 defeats, 30 goals scored and 30 against. On a warm evening, with their backs a hundred yards away from the hard shoulder of the M6 South, 2,408 Pompey fans led the singing that had become customary in most of the grounds visited this season. Walsall laid into Pompey from the start, belying their problems of lowly League position and lack of first-teamers. Hislop had early saves to make from Leitao and Junior.

The Saddlers continued to press forward, with Corica and Junior firing over the bar, and when Kevin Harper, a former Walsall loanee, slipped when trying to make a cross, the home jeers sounded. Pompey were struggling to make an impression. But the wing-back exacted immediate revenge when he scored a spectacular goal on the quarter-hour to improve his credibility even further with some Pompey fans as well as silence the morons who had given him racial abuse two years previously.

Throughout the season, Harper could be classed as the most improved player in a team of Redknapp purchases. Thorough, dependent and with a high level of concentration, his goal oozed the class of a Premiership strike. He collected a cross-field pass just inside Walsall's half and, with a great first touch, rounded two midfielders, sprinted at goal as the Saddlers' defence was caught, used both feet to balance himself, and coolly placed a firm shot past Darren Ward in the Walsall goal. He muted the earlier jeers by turning his back on the Walsall end and pointing to his name on the back of his shirt. It was Pompey's first ever goal at the Bescot Stadium.

Pompey were forced to substitute Yakubu, who limped off clutching his left thigh, and bring on Deon Burton after 20 minutes. It was Pompey who now assumed control and they broke up all Walsall attacks as their confidence grew. Sherwood now took a share of home-fan abuse, as he tussled with Junior and had his protests waved away by the referee. But he too answered with an immediate riposte as he collected a throw-in on the edge of Walsall's penalty area, cleverly beat two defenders with a flick and then clipped a cross to the far post for Todorov to head home his nineteenth goal in the 33rd minute. He nearly scored again when he shot narrowly over the bar, after Festa had taken the ball away from Junior.

Pompey then 'stroked' the ball around the park, playing keep-ball for over a minute, much to the delight of the Pompey fans behind the M6 goal, who greeted each touch with 'Olé'. However, after about twenty passes, the move suddenly

---

Walsall 1
Junior

Portsmouth 2
Harper
Todorov

Job done. Pompey players celebrate Toddy's goal at Walsall.

went wrong as half-time approached. Australian Hayden Foxe, at the heart of Pompey's defence, lost possession in his own area to Junior, who then sprinted 20 yards and, with only Hislop to beat, angled a left-foot strike in off the post. It was careless, but Pompey still led 2-1.

A nervy second half developed, with Walsall dominating the action, but Ward had to pull off a great save to deny Nigel Quashie after 65 minutes, when he exchanged passes with Merson and fired in a 25-yard shot. The game became frenetic in the last 15 minutes with both sides going near; Merson was the more unlucky not to score, when he nearly lost his balance as the ball bobbled towards goal, and Roper raced back to prevent the ball from crossing the line.

With 3 minutes left, referee Mathieson became public enemy number one, as he waved away protests of Hislop punching the ball outside his area. It was a clear infringement, but both the linesman and referee missed it. Pompey's eleventh hard-earned away win had arrived, and a massive 86-point total separated them by 3 from Leicester, who had also won, on 83. The Pompey chants of 'Goodbye to the Nationwide' were getting louder.

Walsall: Ward, Bazeley, Carbon, Roper, Aranalde, Sonner, Corica, Wrack, Samways, Leitao, Junior . Subs: Hay, Zdrillic, M.Harris, Mathias, Barras.
Portsmouth: Hislop, Foxe, Festa, Primus, Harper, Quashie, Sherwood, Merson, Stone, Todorov, Yakubu. Subs: Burton, O'Neil, Diabate, Heikkinen, Kawaguchi.

FROM A JACK TO A KING

Kevin Harper raced 40 yards to score a brilliant solo goal at the Bescot.

Gianluca Festa wins the ball with a balletic movement versus Walsall.

Date: Saturday 12 April 2003
Attendance: 19,524

Referee: David Crick (Surrey)
Man of the Match: Tim Sherwood

During one of Pompey's greatest seasons in history, there had to be a let-down somewhere. It simply wouldn't be Pompey if things were too straightforward. Everything had gone so well – a win over luckless Sheffield Wednesday, bottom of the League, would clinch promotion by virtue of 89 points. The air of expectancy was a little too confident, both on the pitch and off it, as a sell-out crowd crammed into Fratton Park for the first home game in a month. The sun was out, the massive flag passed over the Fratton End seats and Pompey came out to a deafening roar. Many of the crowd had overlooked the problem of Pompey's weak strike force, with Yakubu out injured and Lee Bradbury recalled from his loan spell at Sheffield Wednesday to play against the side he had scored for the previous weekend. It was his first start in a Pompey shirt for sixteen months.

Pompey began nervously, in comparison with Wednesday's squad they had nothing to lose. Defeat for Wednesday, however, would mean Hartlepool visiting Hillsborough next season. Primus was on top form and his alertness frustrated Kuqi with two successive great tackles. But the Owls, winners of a single match away from home all season, looked equally solid at the back Against the run of play, Pompey calmed everyone's nerves on 20 minutes, with Lee Bradbury scoring a fairy-tale goal. Todorov was the schemer; one of his familiar runs down the right beat two defenders, and he reached the byline and cut back a cross which Pressman in the Milton goal could only deflect into the path of Isle of Wight-born striker Bradbury, who slammed it in. Fratton went wild. Promotion was 70 minutes away.

But after a time, curiously, there was still an apprehensive atmosphere in the ground, with 1,000 Owls fans making considerable noise with their four-piece band on the open Milton End. Just before half-time, Shaka Hislop punched a half-chance from Murphy clear to keep Pompey ahead. De Zeeuw was on for Harper when the teams swapped halves, and Harry switched to a back four, with Festa on the left and Primus on the right. Pompey searched for a second goal to put them in the comfort zone, but Todorov's effort slid into the side netting. Pressman saved at Bradbury's feet and Merson shot over the Fratton End bar. Corner after corner came and went, and the atmosphere became edgy.

In the 73rd minute, Owls manager Chris Turner brought on Reddy and Holt, two pairs of fresh legs which turned the game. Pompey's nerves were visibly jangling as the Yorkshire side equalised with 14 minutes left. Primus only half-cleared a high ball into the box, Hislop failed to punch the ball properly and the ball fell to Ashley Westwood, who pushed the ball over the line. 1-1. The Fratton Park faithful were annoyed. Sheffield had not threatened to score, but Pompey had allowed them back in the game and the visitors sensed their tension.

Pompey then contrived to worsen even further – continually giving the ball away. Hislop saved a terrific 25-yard shot from Alan Quinn, and just as everyone thought

Portsmouth 1	Sheffield Wednesday 2
Bradbury	*Westwood*
	Ready

Lee Bradbury: 'Excuse me, I'm scoring for Pompey this week.' Owls defender Lee Bromby looks on.

the game was heading for a draw, Pompey won a free-kick in the 2nd minute of injury time. To add to the frantic nature of Pompey's play, confusion and controversy arose over a freak incident. The referee ordered the free-kick back ten yards to just inside Pompey's own half. Stone kicked the ball back to Festa, but with the Italian defender suffering double vision from a head injury, he merely tapped the ball. Wednesday's Irish forward Michael Reddy, only a yard away when he should have been ten, pounced onto the ball, charged up to the Milton End and put the ball away past Hislop. The referee awarded a goal, much to everyone's amazement. The majority were stunned. Owls fans celebrated. Reddy should have been booked for not being ten yards back – an unnoticed incident that should have disallowed the goal. The whole thing was surreal; oddly, no one complained except Harry Redknapp, and promotion was on ice.

To make matters worse, Leicester City had drawn at Rotherham and knocked Pompey off the top for the first time since August. What a smack in the face. What an afternoon.

Portsmouth: Hislop, Foxe, Festa, Primus, Harper, Quashie, Sherwood, Merson, Stone, Todorov, Bradbury. Subs: De Zeeuw, O'Neil, Diabate, Burton, Kawaguchi.
Sheffield Wednesday: Pressman, D. Smith, Maddix, Bromby, Westwood, Murphy, Haslam, McLaren, Quinn, Kuqi, Owusu. Subs: Reddy, Holt, Evans, Wood, Stringer.

BIG DAY JITTERS

We've scored! Tim Sherwood savours the moment before it all went wrong.

It was asking a lot, but Lee Bradbury did it and scored. But what an end!

Date: Tuesday 15 April 2003
Attendance: 19,221

Referee: Brian Curson (Leicestershire)
Man of the Match: Svetoslav Todorov

A warm April evening after a sunny bright day was the perfect complement to the feeling at Fratton Park for this rearranged fixture and Pompey's second chance, still with four more games to play, to win promotion. It was an evening of raw nerves, unbridled passion and late drama. The combined partnership of Yakubu and Toddy was over, with 'the Yak' out for the rest of the season and, lacking the fast-paced skills of Matthew Taylor and Kevin Harper, Harry Redknapp struggled to field a side of regular first-teamers for this important game.

All four sides of the ground housed Pompey fans again, and their loud singing and chanting helped coax the players into performing at their best. The atmosphere seemed buoyant, relaxed and less fraught than Saturday, as the Fratton End burst into a selection of '70s and '80s chants to stir up the whole ground into a secure belief that Pompey were going to do something special tonight. Visitors Burnley, safe from relegation, were nearing the end of a wretched season that had seen them concede 77 goals, and they lost striker Papadopoulos after 9 minutes with a spine injury. Just 3 minutes later, Clarets defender Dean West tripped Festa in the box; a perfect chance for Pompey to assert the lead, but the normally reliable penalty-taker Paul Merson unbelievably struck the crossbar, and Lee Bradbury's follow-up from the rebound was cleared by McGregor.

But there was no indulgence in self-pity – the crowd just got louder in their support. Pompey were doing it the hard way – again! Several more chances went begging, Merson and Todorov trying their utmost with shots which flew just past the post. Pompey's rhythm and cohesion were missing again, and although Burnley never looked capable of scoring, the match looked a certain 0-0. In the second half, news of Sheffield's goal against Forest merely turned up the crescendo of noise in the ground. Pericard replaced Bradbury on 70 minutes, and it was the Juventus loanee whose pass 3 minutes later led to a historic win. The Frenchman side-passed to Quashie, who hit a low, angled drive into the 6-yard box, and who else but leading scorer Svetoslav Todorov was in perfect position to slot the ball home for goal number twenty. He dived head first into the rows of seats in the Fratton End to celebrate! The relief around the ground was immense; fans hugged each other and the moment was enormous.

This time, happily, there was no twist or cruel late equaliser. Burnley didn't spoil the party. The wall of sound which erupted on the final whistle was almost deafening. Deep emotion in thousands of Pompey fans' hearts poured out as 5,000 people ignored warnings and invaded the pitch. Once cleared, the team emerged carrying a banner, stating 'We're going up', and a lap of honour of sorts followed. Chairman Milan Mandaric held another large banner aloft in the directors' box proclaiming 'Step aside, Saints, Pompey are in the Premiership'. 89 points had done it. Across the whole city, chanting and car horns were heard, as fans danced in the

Portsmouth 1	Burnley 0
Todorov	

'Yes, sir, that's my twentieth!' Todorov seals Pompey's promotion.

streets to celebrate a return to the elite; a League in which Pompey had established themselves from 1927 to 1959 and had flirted with for just one season in 1987/88 under Alan Ball.

After the match, which many found mentally exhausting, amid all the signings and talk of next season, there was time to reflect on the two main characters who had achieved the dream far quicker than expected: Milan Mandaric, whose millions had kept Pompey alive after administration difficulties and who paid the wages to entice some of the more experienced players in to the club, and Harry Redknapp, with wise assistance from Jim Smith and Kevin Bond, who had worked a miracle; turning round a club who had finished in the bottom eight for the last eight seasons, using his tremendous football knowledge and tactical awareness to build a Pompey team in twelve months and win promotion in just 42 games.

The much-awaited news filtered around the country and around the world as Pompey made the national headlines – thousands of fans who could not be among the crowd celebrated in their own way, as the traditional and much-loved name of Pompey at last was the subject of a happy event again.

Portsmouth: Hislop, Primus, Foxe, De Zeeuw, Stone, Festa, Sherwood, Quashie, Merson, Todorov, Bradbury. Subs: Pericard, O'Neil, Diabate, Harper, Kawaguchi.
Burnley: Michopoulos, West, Gnohere, Davis, McGregor, Weller, Branch, Moore, G. Taylor, R. Blake, Papadopolos. Subs: Maylett, O'Neill, Chaplow, Pilkington, Armstrong.

HOT TODDY

One of many Pompey flags waved on the night Pompey won promotion back to the top flight.

Opposite: Pompey's Bulgarian international, who finished as the club's top scorer and was the leading marksman in Division One with 26 goals.

Date: Good Friday 18 April 2003

Attendance: 29,396

Referee: Eddie Wolstenholme (Blackburn)

Man of the Match: Tim Sherwood

A combination of a promotion hangover, tired legs, no proper training and too tight a fixture schedule led to Pompey suffering their worst defeat of the season. The squad were psychologically drained – and it was not a drink-related hangover. Sky TV had brought the much-awaited Easter Saturday fixture forward to a ghastly Friday tea-time start, which gave Pompey just two days to prepare. On one of those, the players could not train as the Southampton University ground gates were locked.

An unchanged Pompey team walked out onto a splendid Portman Road pitch to play a club who had been relegated from the Premiership the previous season and got off to a poor start in the Nationwide, but who were now chasing a play-off place. The largest attendance of the season roared Ipswich on from the start in what was always going to be a tricky game, but it was made more difficult by Pompey's mid-week mathematical promotion and an Ipswich side fired up to secure 3 points. England Under-21 striker Marcus Bent, who cost Ipswich £3 million – more than the entire Pompey team – tore into Pompey's defence within 5 minutes and shot narrowly wide. After 10 minutes, the Tractor Boys went ahead. De Zeeuw played a ball across the pitch straight to Reuser, who ran at Pompey's defence and, from 25 yards, buried a brilliant low shot past Hislop.

The Pompey squad looked jaded, and their game was littered with mistakes. On 27 minutes, Miller fed Richards down the left – De Zeeuw tried to reach him, but Miller had run in on the overlap to smash the ball in from 8 yards to double Ipswich's lead. Just 3 minutes later, Pompey's army of 2,200 fans had hardly got over the shock when danger-man Tommy Miller caused havoc again. The former Ipswich schoolboy delivered a fine pass to Counago, who tricked his way past De Zeeuw and beat Hislop from a tight angle, firing the ball into the roof of the net for 3-0.

It could have got worse. Gianluca Festa, who had earlier forced Ipswich 'keeper Andy Marshall to make a fine save around the post from 25 yards, was very fortunate not to receive Pompey's first red card of the season. Already booked, he twice appeared to elbow Reuser in the face in a challenge for the ball, which the referee chose to ignore.

It was Pompey's worst half of the season, and they were looking a mere shadow of the side who had beaten Burnley a few days earlier. But for the concentration of Foxe, Primus and Sherwood, the score could have been higher. The second half produced stronger commitment, as Pompey held their line well and defended stoutly. Sherwood, booed by Ipswich fans for his Norwich past, sparked up Pompey's midfield, before three substitutions were made to preserve some legs for another match on Monday. Pericard, O'Neil and Harper replaced Bradbury, Merson and De Zeeuw, and both O'Neil and Pericard looked livelier in the last

---

Ipswich Town 3
Reuser, Miller
Counago

Portsmouth 0

Heads you win. Nigel Quashie in an aerial battle with Ipswich striker Tommy Miller.

half-hour than the rest of the team put together, as they displayed some hard and inventive running.

With 15 minutes to go, losing in their gold away strip for only the second time in the League, Pompey's noisy army of fans turned up the volume of sound as they had done on Tuesday night. Paying £23 a ticket, they were determined to enjoy themselves after miserable bank holiday traffic on the A12 had delayed their journey. It had taken two solid hours to travel just fifty-two miles from the Dartford Tunnel east to Ipswich.

Pompey music factotum John Westwood clambered onto a corporate box roof beneath them to single-handedly lead an uninterrupted chorus of 'Top of the League, 'Arry and Jim', which fired up the atmosphere around the whole ground, causing even the linesman to scratch his head as he wondered what the commotion above him was. At the end, both Ipswich and Pompey fans applauded each other – Ipswich had moved to within a point of a play-off place, and Pompey's entourage moved quicker along the A12 in the knowledge that they still had 3 games left to win the title they so deserved. This was the first time Pompey had not scored in a first-team match since the game against Reading on 7 December.

Ipswich Town: Marshall, Wilnis, Holland, Gaardsoe, Makin, Richards, Reuser, Magilton, Miller, Counago, M. Bent. Subs: Wright, Westlake, Armstrong, Bowditch, Pullen.
Portsmouth: Hislop, Foxe, Festa, Primus, De Zeeuw, Quashie, Sherwood, Merson, Stone, Todorov, Bradbury. Subs: Pericard, O'Neil, Harper, Diabate, Kawaguchi.

PERICARD ROYAL FLUSH

Date: Easter Monday 21 April 2003
Attendance: 19,535

Referee: George Cain (Bootle)
Man of the Match: Vincent Pericard

Over the weekend, the sly Foxes had beaten Brighton to go top above Pompey by a point. But their Easter Monday match, an awkward-looking trip to Bramall Lane, kicked off before Pompey started, and loud cheers from public houses around the periphery of Fratton Park could be heard as the Blades scored an injury-time winner. That news gave the Pompey dressing-room the perfect platform from which to run out and defeat Royal Berkshire opponents Reading – a tricky fixture for Pompey. Reading, the surprise team of the division after Pompey since their immediate rise from Division Two, had won 11 away matches and conceded few goals.

Two players returned to Pompey's XI who were to turn the game – wing-back Kevin Harper slotted in neatly, and Vincent Pericard, knee injury mended, ousted Lee Bradbury. A weekend of rest for the Pompey team after the Ipswich result, together with fresh legs, provided an entertaining spectacle, as good as any this season, for a near-capacity attendance – just twenty-four turnstile clicks short of the highest. Shirt-sleeves were adequate for the massive crowd, who were soon chanting Harper's name as he charged alone into the penalty area in the first few minutes. Indeed, it was the little Scotsman who was involved in Pompey's opener on 19 minutes. Harper took the ball down into the box again, and crossed for Vincent Pericard to hit the back of the net with a low, angled shot. His return to the side could not have been better timed, with Yakubu and Taylor both missing.

As the game wore on, it was Reading who looked like Pompey at Portman Road. They had endured an exhausting Good Friday win over Forest, and today they looked nothing like play-off contenders. Pompey were on top and underlined their superiority just on the stroke of half-time. Nigel Quashie had a goal disallowed for offside and Hayden Foxe headed a free-kick narrowly wide, but when Todorov won a through-ball from Sherwood, the Bulgarian demonstrated his well-developed swivel, shook off two Reading defenders and cut the ball back for Pericard to hit with his left foot, at the second attempt, into the net. It was the Frenchman's tenth goal of the season, and his first brace for Pompey.

The Berkshire side chased the game in the second half, and their goal chances were reduced to Steve Stone blocking out Luke Chadwick and Shaka Hislop denying Nicky Shorey. Royals defender Adrian Williams then took a turn to block a shot, this time from Todorov on the line, but, happily, Pompey's leading marksman was not to leave the pitch without scoring. His hard graft was typified in the 71st minute when he lost his marker, sprinted away from others and side-footed a classy goal past Hahnemann in the Fratton goal. He nearly scored another before the end, but Pompey fans gave a bigger cheer to Kevin Harper as he received a standing ovation with 5 minutes left. It was fully deserved and quite something of a turnaround from the same fans who had once booed him.

Portsmouth 3
Pericard (2)
Todorov

Reading 0

The creative running and intelligent ball-play of Vincent Pericard made an important contribution to Pompey's promotion.

On the whistle, Pompey then left the field to more standing applause from their adoring supporters; this team had just broken the club record of points won – a massive 92 – beating their 91 total in 1983 when they won the Third Division title. This whetted the appetite to finish the job, break the goals scored record of 91 from their 89 already netted and win some much-needed silverware to place in the trophy cabinet up in the boardroom. By supper-time, when Wolves had beaten Norwich 3-0, it became clear that Pompey needed 4 points from their 2 remaining games to clinch their first ever Division One title of the newly-structured leagues. Their heavy goalscoring against Derby, Millwall and Coventry had helped to give Pompey a goal difference that was 13 goals superior to Leicester's, who were now 2 points behind.

Portsmouth: Hislop, Primus, Foxe, Festa, Stone, Harper, Sherwood, Quashie, Merson, Pericard, Todorov. Subs: De Zeeuw, Diabate, O'Neil, Burton, Kawaguchi.
Reading: Hahnemann, Murty, A.Williams, S. Brown, Shorey, Chadwick, Harper, Newman, Hughes, Little, Forster. Subs: Mackie, Henderson, Salako, Cureton, Ashdown.

TODOROV TRAPS TITLE

Date: Sunday 27 April 2003
Attendance: 19,420

Referee: Richard Beeby (Northants)
Man of the Match: Svetoslav Todorov

Match number 45. Yet another Sky TV appearance for Pompey meant another blank Saturday, as the match was crammed into an already full schedule of televised games on Sunday to really mess up everyone's weekend, with an unorthodox 6.30 p.m. kick-off. However, the importance of the game ensured that Fratton Park was a sea of colour, as flags, hats and horns appeared to ensure a well-remembered last home game of the season. There had been plenty of 'last home games' in recent seasons which were just as important, but at the other end of the table. The excitement was augmented by Leicester failing to beat Norwich earlier in the afternoon, so Pompey only needed to win the match to clinch the title.

Unchanged from Monday, Pompey faced a mid-table Yorkshire side who had a good reputation for defeating several top clubs. Unfashionable, physical and uncompromising were three words used to describe Rotherham. They had a duty not to lie down. Their tackles were fierce and their defence towered high. Pompey lost the toss – not a good omen as they kicked towards the Fratton End first. No one could have predicted another five goals all in one half, but the referee started them off when he saw fit to give Pompey a penalty after 11 minutes, when Todorov fell debatably near Branston, and up stepped Paul Merson to score a spot-kick for his first ever goal at the Fratton End. Just 5 minutes later, Rotherham centre half Branston exacted revenge as he darted between blue shirts from a Shaun Barker throw to side-foot home. 1-1.

End-to-end action followed. It was a numerical moment for Todorov when Pericard latched on to Steve Stone's ball played down the flank and crossed low for the Bulgarian to dodge his opponent and score his twenty-second goal of the season in the 22nd minute. But just before the half-hour, the persistent Millers were level again. Another centre half, Chris Swailes, out-jumped Shaka Hislop from a corner to fire home hard into the Milton net to make the score 2-2.

Harper sadly limped off with a recurrence of his groin injury, and Dutch warhorse Arjan De Zeeuw came on. Festa moved to emergency wing-back and, in injury time, his pass lead to another Pompey goal. Noticing Quashie in space, he crossed for Nigel to nod the ball back to Pericard, who linked well with Todorov to smash in a low shot from close range. 3-2. Fratton Park erupted. It was the same score as at Millmoor in October, and befitting for Pompey's leading scorer to break the club record for goals in a season by scoring Pompey's ninety-second of the campaign.

The second half was just as fraught; Rotherham's unusual style was to keep banging the ball towards the net for it to then ricochet several times off anybody's legs, in the hope of a third equaliser. Merson, and then surprise substitute Yakubu, went close, before Millers midfielder Alan Lee placed a header just wide. At 8.13 p.m., inconsistent referee Mr Beeby ended the match and the players tried to run

---

Portsmouth 3
Merson (penalty)
Todorov (2)

Rotherham United 2
Branston
Swailes

A traditional ticker-tape welcome from the Fratton End as the teams take the field.

Portsmouth: Hislop, Primus, Foxe, Festa, Harper, Quashie, Sherwood, Merson, Stone, Todorov, Pericard. Subs: De Zeeuw, Yakubu, Diabate, O'Neil, Kawaguchi.
Rotherham United: Gray, Barker, McIntosh, Swailes, Branston, Sedgwick, Lee, Barker, Daws, Talbot, Hurst. Subs: Warne, Monkhouse, Robins, Hudson, Politt.

TODOROV TRAPS TITLE

What a turnaround for a club who regularly finished in the bottom half each season.

for safety but, much against the opinion of the majority, morons invaded the pitch to delay the celebrations. Pompey had done it! League champions. They had been there all season and had now beaten their close pursuers to achieve glory – sweet revenge for 1949 and 1993.

When the pitch was clear, the real moment of belief in hearts and in heads came into view. Two Nationwide officials carried the podium stage onto the centre of the pitch for the team to assemble on, and the banana-shaped sign which followed, affixed to the stanchions, brought a tear to many an eye when they read 'Portsmouth FC, Division One Champions'. With one game to go, Pompey had won the title – at home for a change. The songs and chants were bellowed out with laudable force. The team re-emerged, and Paul Merson sank to his knees and hailed the Fratton End fans. What a night, what a season, what a club.

Few would argue that Pompey, top for all but a few weeks, deserved it. Announcements were made and the magnificent large trophy brought out by two of Portsmouth's oldest stewards, Pompey's thousands clapped and cheered until their hands and throats were sore. Even some of the 134 Rotherham supporters stayed to join in the party and enjoy the champagne being thrown around. It was Pompey's first silverware for twenty years and, with the quality of football played, what a well-deserved trophy it was. Those who were there had little sleep that night. Well done, Pompey – how proud we are.

The man who engineered it all – Harry Redknapp, Pompey's manager.

COUP DE GRACE

Date: Sunday 4 May 2003
Attendance: 19,088

Referee: Steve Baines (Chesterfield)
Man of the Match: Svetoslav Todorov/Steve Stone

A queue for the 7,000 tickets that Bradford City provided beyond their normal allocation stretched long and early at Fratton Park, weeks before the game was played. Even with the Championship secured, the demand for tickets to Pompey's last match of the season outweighed supply. Uncannily, playing against a side they'd had several last-day scrapes with in previous seasons, Bradford turned blue and white from dawn until dusk as the legions of Pompey fans turned Manningham into a one-day street festival.

In the ground, Pompey fans were housed on three sides of Valley Parade. A carnival-style street party engulfed the stadium with flags, air-horns, streamers and ticker tape, as Pompey welcomed the League champions out onto the pitch, all wearing white boots. It was a fulfilled promise to Gianluca Festa, who part-owns the Italian footwear company A-line, to wear them once Pompey were promoted and in his last game before he returned to Italy. De Zeeuw was back in for Harper, and Yakubu, who had recovered quicker than expected, was surprisingly favoured in place of Pericard. The only disappointment of the day was City's ground capacity of 25,000 – all those empty seats could have been filled by Pompey fans.

After a minute's silence, observed in memory of the tragic ground fire eighteen years previously, the home side were unlucky not to score twice through Robert Molenaar with close headers, and leading scorer Andy Gray curled a free-kick just wide. Were Pompey treating the game as a knees-up? No, it was the unlikely, but appropriate figure of Festa, on his farewell appearance, who opened the scoring after 20 minutes. Running on to a half-chance, the Italian struck his first, and only, goal for Pompey by virtue of a lucky deflection off City midfielder Jorgenson. But it was no less than he deserved for his tremendous performances in 27 games over the season. Pompey then continued to play 'pass the ball' for the rest of the half, as they enjoyed a mid-afternoon stroll. Chances fell to Quashie, who side-footed over the bar, Stone, who narrowly shot wide, and Yakubu, who let rip from 20 yards, but none of them went in. City, woefully starved of some regulars through injury or departure, almost stood back and watched with admiration.

The second half saw an explosive hat-trick develop in the space of just 10 minutes. With Bradford's defence caught square, Steve Stone crossed the ball for Todorov, who swept in his twenty-fourth goal of a memorable season in the 48th minute. Just 2 minutes later, Paul Merson found space away from Francis and passed to Yakubu Ayegbeni, whose deep cross connected neatly with Toddy. With his usual precision, he clinically thumped a right-footer in to make it 3-0. A further 8 minutes later, the Bulgarian was tackled inside the box by David Wetherall – a decision that was flagged down by the linesman. Referee Baines, a former Bradford City player, awarded a penalty to everyone's surprise. Todorov understandably wanted to take it instead of Merson. The Bulgarian duly sent City 'keeper Davison

---

Bradford City 0

Portsmouth 5
Festa, Todorov (3, including 1 penalty)
Stone

the wrong way for his twenty-sixth goal and overtook Forest striker David Johnson as the division's top marksman.

Steve Stone, who had worked hard with uncompromising energy, then earned himself a deserved goal in the 67th minute from a Tim Sherwood pass and Todorov flick-on. Five goals away from home again, Pompey fans were delirious and almost punch-drunk with satisfaction: 'We want six', they bayed from the main stand. City fans underneath replied 'We want one'. As a reward for his season-long patience without a first-team game, Japanese goalkeeper Yoshi Kawaguchi replaced Shaka Hislop at half-time (so as not to spoil Shaka's full house of 46 games) and earned applause all round Valley Parade with a fingertip save to push away Uhlenbeek's powerful shot against a post. City tried again, when Gray pounded a header onto the crossbar and Yoshi saved at Danny Forrest's feet, but it was not to be, and another clean sheet was recorded.

Was this Utopia? This first hat-trick for a Pompey player this season followed the achievements of two 5-0 away wins in the same season; no one sent off in nine months; a club record of 98 points; a club record of 97 goals; a club record-equalling 12 away wins; just 6 defeats in 46 games; Pompey's seventh championship in their history; and dazzling one-touch football that was the talk of the division. Finishing 6 points above the hoof-it style of Leicester and 18 points above the Blades, Pompey were back in the best League in the world. It was indeed Utopia, and it still took some believing as we sped back down the M1 back to Hampshire.

Gianluca Festa played an important part for Pompey in his 27 games, and scored in his last match before returning to Italy.

Bradford City: Davison, Uhlenbeek, Molenaar, Wetherall, Bower, Jorgenson, Francis, Muirhead, Myers, Forrest, A.Gray. Subs: Penford, Pen Heuvel, Fanasy, Wright, Magnusson.

Portsmouth: Hislop, Primus, Foxe, De Zeeuw, Stone, Sherwood, Quashie, Festa, Merson, Yakubu, Todorov. Subs: Kawaguchi, Diabate, O'Neil, Burton, Pericard.

2002/03 Portsmouth Statistics

Most wins in a season   29
Previous best was 27 in 1961/62 and 1982/83

Total goals scored   97
Previous best was 91 in 1979/80

Highest points total   98
Previous best was 91 in 1982/83

Most away goals in a season   45
Previous best was 39 in 1961/62

Most away wins in a season   12
Previous best was 12 in 1961/62

Fewest defeats in a season   6
Previous best was 7 in 1921/22 and 1923/24

Fewest defeats away in a season   3
Previous best was 4 in 1921/22 and 1984/85

Most consecutive wins   7
Previous best was 7 in 1982/83

Cup games not included. Statistics include League games
only from 1920/21, consisting of 40, 42 and 46 games.

Player	League Apps	Cup Apps	Sub Apps	Total Goals
Shaka Hislop	46	3	0	0
Paul Merson	44	3	1	12
Svetoslav Todorov	43	3	2	26
Nigel Quashie	42	2	0	6
Linvoy Primus	38	3	1	1
Matt Taylor	35	3	0	7
Arjan De Zeeuw	35	1	3	1
Hayden Foxe	30	1	2	1
Gianluca Festa	27	2	0	1
Kevin Harper	21	2	17	4
Vincent Pericard	18	1	16	10
Steve Stone	18	1	0	5
Lassina Diabate	16	1	9	0
Tim Sherwood	17	0	0	1
Gary O'Neil	11	1	21	3
Carl Robinson	11	1	5	0
Yakubu Ayegbeni	12	0	2	7
Deon Burton	11	0	5	4
Paul Ritchie	8	1	4	0
Jason Crowe	7	1	8	4
Mark Burchill	4	1	15	4
Richard Hughes	4	1	2	0
Stathis Tavlaridis	3	1	1	0
Lee Bradbury	3	0	0	1
Eddie Howe	1	0	0	0
Markus Heikkinen	0	0	2	0
Carl Tiler	0	0	2	0
Yoshi Kawaguchi	0	0	1	0
Lewis Buxton	0	0	1	0

POMPEY – DIVISION ONE CHAMPIONS, 2002/03

	Name	P	HOME					AWAY					GD	PTS
			W	D	L	F	A	W	D	L	F	A		
1	**Portsmouth**	**46**	**17**	**3**	**3**	**52**	**22**	**12**	**8**	**3**	**45**	**23**	**52**	**98**
2	Leicester City	46	16	5	2	40	12	10	9	4	33	28	33	92
3	Sheffield United	46	13	7	3	38	23	10	9	4	34	29	20	80
4	Reading	46	13	3	7	33	21	10	4	9	28	25	15	79
5	Wolverhampton Wanderers	46	9	10	4	40	19	12	1	10	41	28	37	76
6	Nottingham Forest	46	14	7	2	57	23	6	7	10	25	27	32	74
7	Ipswich Town	46	10	5	8	49	39	9	8	6	31	25	16	70
8	Norwich City	46	14	4	5	36	17	5	8	10	24	32	11	69
9	Millwall	46	11	6	6	34	32	8	3	12	25	37	-10	66
10	Wimbledon	46	11	6	6	39	28	6	8	9	34	45	3	65
11	Gillingham	46	10	6	7	33	31	6	8	9	23	34	-9	62
12	Preston North End	46	11	7	5	44	29	5	6	12	24	41	-2	61
13	Watford	46	11	5	7	33	26	6	4	13	21	44	-16	60
14	Crystal Palace	46	8	10	5	29	17	6	7	10	30	35	7	59
15	Rotherham United	46	8	9	6	27	25	7	5	11	35	37	0	59
16	Burnley	46	10	4	9	35	44	5	6	12	30	45	-24	55
17	Walsall	46	10	3	10	34	34	5	6	12	23	35	-12	54
18	Derby County	46	9	5	9	33	32	6	2	15	22	42	-19	52
19	Bradford City	46	7	8	8	27	35	7	2	14	24	38	-22	52
20	Coventry City	46	6	6	11	23	31	6	8	9	23	31	-16	50
21	Stoke City	46	9	6	8	25	25	3	6	12	20	44	-24	50
22	Sheffield Wednesday	46	7	7	9	25	32	3	9	11	27	41	-17	46
23	Brighton and Hove Albion	46	7	6	10	29	31	4	6	13	20	36	-18	45
24	Grimsby Town	46	5	6	12	26	39	4	6	13	22	46	-37	39